MAGIC BOOKS

& Paper Toys

by Esther K Smith

illos Liz Zanis

photos Amy Kalyn Sims

POTTER
CRAFT
New York

Flip Books, E-Z Pop-Ups & Other Paper Playthings to Amaze & Delight

This is dedicated to the ones I love—you know who you are!

Thanks again and again to everyone I thanked in **How to Make Books**, and thanks to everyone who bought **How to Make Books**, to Jessica Stockton Bagnulo of McNally Robinson and all booksellers who've sold it, to Michael Kindness and the rest of the RH sales team, to Melissa Bonventre, Rosy Ngo, Lauren Shakely, Marysarah Quinn, Alice Peisch, Katherine Sungarian, Erica Smith, Erin Slonaker, Isa Loundon, Christina Schoen, Thom O'Hearn, Amy Sly and Chi Ling Moy. Thanks a jillion to my illustrator Liz Zanis and photographer Amy Kalyn Sims, to Alice Austin, Susan Happersett, and Polly Faust for their contributions. Thanks also to AA Bronson and Printed Matter, Laurie Whitehill Chong and RISD, Landria Shack and Pyramid Atlantic, Scott Durkin, Georgia Luna, Sam Potts, Matt Danzico, Susan Landry, Kyle Forester, Richard Olson for his rubberstamp collection, and especially to my Splendid web angel Lissi Erwin.

Copyright © 2008 by Esther K. Smith
Photographs copyright © 2008 Amy Kalyn Sims
Illustrations copyright © 2008 Liz Zanis

POTTER
CRAFT

Published in the United States by Potter Craft,
an imprint of the Crown Publishing Group,
a division of Random House, Inc., New York.
www.clarksonpotter.com
www.pottercraft.com

POTTER CRAFT and colophon is a registered
trademark of Random House, Inc.

Library of Congress Cataloging-in-Publication Data
is available upon request.

ISBN 978-0-307-40709-2

Printed in China

Design by Chi Ling Moy
and Purgatory Pie Press: Esther K. Smith & Dikko Faust

10 9 8 7 6 5 4 3 2 1

First Edition

CONTENTS

Introduction: Magic Books

These projects are easy and fun to make. Don't even read this—just grab a bone folder and get started!

You just need a few simple tools: good, sharp scissors (use the good scissors for paper—I give you permission!), a bone folder (or fingernail), linen thread and strong darning needles, and an awl for the books. And some adhesive—glue sticks, double-stick tape, paste, or glue. Try them all to see what you like. *Never* use rubber cement or masking tape—their acidity destroys paper. Be careful with spray mount. Those tiny particles go everywhere—into your cup of coffee, into the air, into your lungs. And when you burnish with a bone folder, protect your work with clean waste paper to avoid that bone folder shine.

My approach is to show you some approaches. Most projects will take just a few minutes to try. Make preliminary models ("dummies") from scraps and recycled stuff—junk mail, cereal boxes, the backs of paper from your printer. These are your doodles on the back of an envelope. (In this book, projects attributed to EKS are quick pieces I've made as teaching demos.) When you are comfortable with the basics, design your pieces and choose your materials. Buy expensive handmade papers, continue recycling, or use something in between—nice art paper or high-end office paper.

Find inspiration everywhere—from shoe boxes (see how they're made!) to magazine ads. (There was a giveaway paper thing in a Polly-O™ string cheese bag when my kids were little—can't remember where I put it, but I know I didn't throw it out!). Go to museums, libraries' special collections and historic societies. Liz Zanis, who illustrated this book and made many project samples, works in the Prints Study Room at the Metropolitan Museum of Art in New York City. It is open to the public by appointment. You can sit at a table with Rembrandt and Picasso prints. I went to see the Anonymous stuff: the valentines, cigarette enclosures, and the Shaker women's paper art.

Start making! Have fun. Some projects will flatten to send in an envelope (if you can remember what stamps cost). Imagine getting a paper toy in the mail! Amaze your friends with these little gifts, stocking stuffers, promo pieces, invitations. I wish I could see what you make.

Remember to *use your good scissors and fold with verve!*

Purgatory Pie Press datebooks: "Leap Year of Fate," "Time is No Object," "MotoLog."
Letterpress from linoleum cuts and hand set metal type, long-stitched into leather covers.

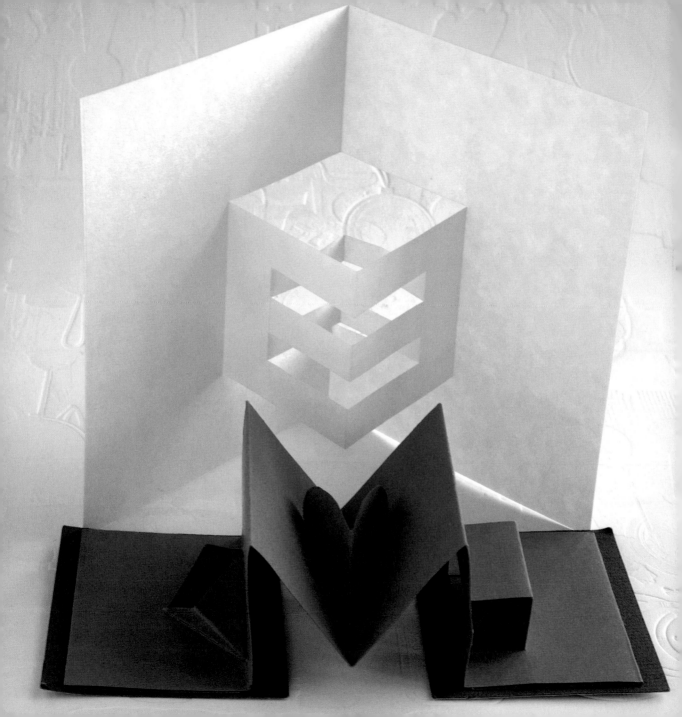

Two basic folds and a cut or two are all you need to make many symmetrical pop-ups. (OK, really you CAN do more cuts.) Beyond these simple approaches are much more complex movable and pop-up forms. But these are my favorites, the ones with the most bang for your buck (as a mother said of the gigantic Day-Glo orange plastic toy vehicle she gave at a birthday party we attended in the burbs).

Don't let yourself get frustrated. If one thing doesn't work for you, something else will. Come back to it later, when it makes more sense. I love teaching, because I get to see brains at work. Some students pick up on a form so fast that they have gone to the next step before I finish explaining the first, but another technique puzzles them. Other students take longer to understand. But most important, when they really get it, the slower students come up with something very interesting that the faster students haven't taken the time to figure out. Go at your own pace. It's not a race. It's what you do with it in the end that's important. Remember, you are doing this for fun. (The fame and profit will all fall into place later.)

Pop-Up Basics

Remember: Fold with verve! It's only paper, but put your weight into it. And put your strength into your folds—a work surface you can really lean into is the best. (Think kitchen counter, if clearing it isn't harder than building a new one!) But whatever surface you are working on, sitting at your kitchen table or your desk at work or school, or even leaning on a book on your lap, crease your folds well. I recommend that you pick up a bone folder, but for thin paper you can burnish with your fingernail, paperclip, or anything that doesn't mark your paper as you rub over your preliminary folds to make them sharp.

These basic pop-ups start with the same pre-fold, so make a bunch of them to have ready as you play with the form. You can use that pile of one-sided printer paper that you are recycling if you like. It's easiest to do these on paper that is a little heavier, but is still easy to fold.

Preliminary Pop-Up Pre-Fold Blanks

This preliminary pre-fold makes your pop-ups easier to pop. Fold a bunch of these from one-sided printer paper and keep them handy for these simple pop-ups. All you have to do is fold your paper in half and burnish with a bone folder. Then reverse the fold, tuning it back the other way, and burnish again.

FOR ALL THE POP-UPS, YOU WILL NEED
Pre-folded paper blanks (see above)
Bone folder (or substitute)
Colored pencils, markers, or rubber stamps to embellish
Scissors (as needed—though you can tear if you really want to)

One Fold, No Cuts Basic Triangle

1. With your pop-up blank, fold a diagonal, from around the center of the fold to near the center of the top or bottom, as shown. It will form a triangle. Burnish.

2. Open, and fold it back the other way, reversing your fold. Burnish again. Unfold.

3. Now open your pre-fold partway to form a tent, both edges on the table, fold up. Hold the tent with one hand. Use your other hand to push that triangle inside out, into the tent. Close the paper and burnish.

4. Open and close gently to see the triangle pop up and move.

Voilà! An instant evergreen tree. Color it green and add some star stickers and it can be an Christmas card. Or dot with polka dots to make it into the skirt of a party dress. Turn it around and it's a sconce. Cut a curved top for a valentine.

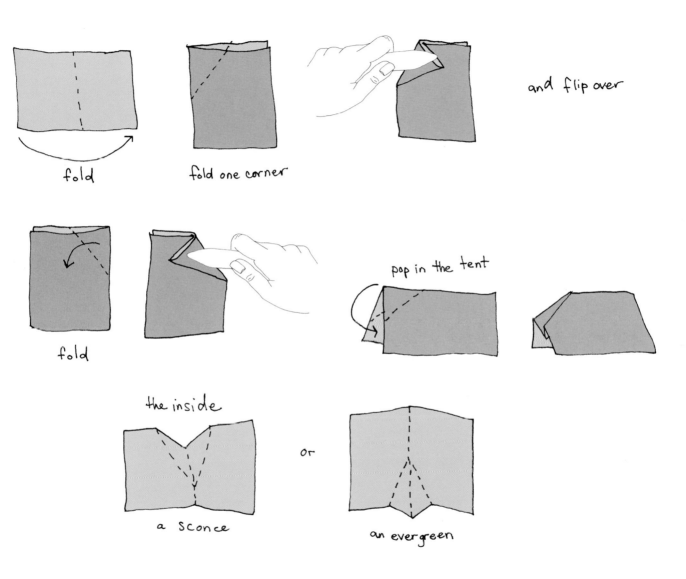

fold

fold one corner

and flip over

fold

pop in the tent

the inside

a sconce

or

an evergreen

One Cut, Two Folds! (Basic Froggy Mouth Pop-Up)

1. Start with your basic pop-up pre-fold.

2. Cut a perpendicular line through your fold near the middle.

3. Fold 2 triangles, one above and one below your cut. Your triangles points should be a little in from the top and bottom.

4. Burnish the fold, then open it.

5. Fold it back the other way, burnish, and open it.

6. Form your pop-up tent—the edges of the paper on the table and the preliminary fold up.

7. Supporting the tent with one hand, push the pop-ups down with your other hand.

8. Close, burnish, and open and shut gently to be sure it moves well. Try saying "FEED ME!!!!," à la *Little Shop of Horrors*.

You've just made the froggy mouth. Draw some eyes on it and you've got a face. It's fun to make these and give them to little kids to draw on. Have them use pens or markers instead of crayons so they won't smear. But whatever's handy will keep them amused (my mother-in-law always had drawing supplies handy to keep children occupied during church—imagine what her kids would have made if she'd had some pop-ups handy). And if you are ever desperate, you can tear instead of cut. These pop-ups are one-sided, so they are a great way to recycle more of that computer printer by-product.

Variations

There is no reason that your cut in step 1 must be straight. This time make your cut a gentle curve a little into the paper one-quarter from the bottom. Make your triangle folds very shallow. It's a harder fold. Burnish and pop as above. It's a more natural mouth. You can cut a sort of nostril cut just above the mouth and fold a nose. Draw or collage some eyes (eyes cut from fashion magazines look interesting and weird on these and almost human). You can even draw other details like hair or ears.

Paper Grain

Paper "wants" to fold in one direction (with the grain) more than the other. It's not impossible to fold against the grain. To test paper grain, try bending the paper in both directions and see which seems to offer less resistance. Or, cut little swatches from your paper, indicating with a pencil line which way the swatch fits onto the larger sheet. Dampen the paper and see how it curls when it dries. It curls in the direction of the grain (as it likes to fold). This tells you how the larger sheet of paper will fold best.

one cut and two folds
(or a froggy mouth)

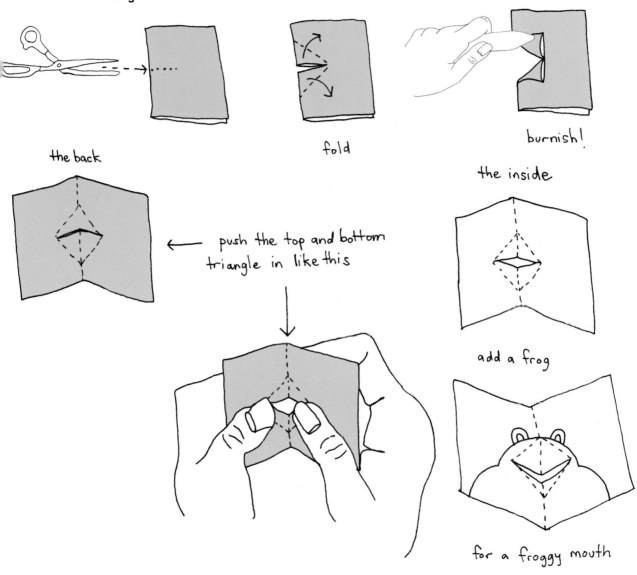

fold

burnish!

the back

the inside

← push the top and bottom triangle in like this

add a frog

for a froggy mouth

Two Cuts, One Fold (Basic Box Pop-Up)

1. Cut two horizontal snips, about 1" wide and about 2" apart through the fold as shown.

2. Fold in the paper between these two cuts. Burnish. Fold back the other way, reversing your fold, burnish again, and unfold.

3. Open your basic folded blank into a tent shape, as shown, and push down the folded piece. Close and burnish the pop-up. Open and close gently to check that your pop-up box functions.

This box pop-up doesn't have to be a box. Its only requirement is that the folded hinge be big enough to support the pop-up. You can draw a half circle across the fold and cut the top and bottom, making a flat hinge on the side. Or cut the top and bottom in any shape you like. Try something abstract and wiggly. Just leave a big enough place to fold for a hinge.

DO NOT cut more than halfway through your paper—if you do, your folded piece will stick out the other side, though if that happens, you can hide the piece sticking out with a larger cover.

Keep in mind: These do not have to be cute, literal pop-ups. You can use them in an abstract, sculptural way. Think about pop-ups architecturally.

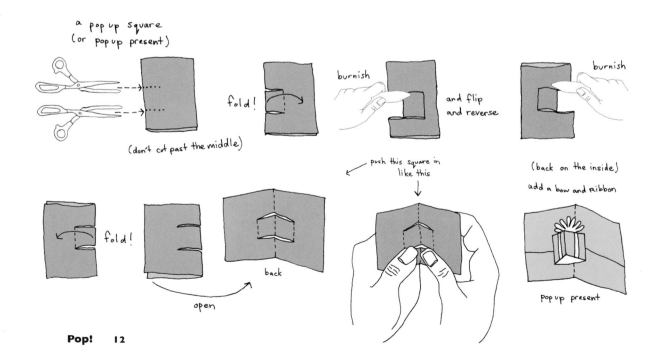

a pop up square
(or pop up present)

(don't cut past the middle)

fold!

burnish

and flip
and reverse

burnish

fold!

open

back

push this square in
like this

(back on the inside)

add a bow and ribbon

pop up present

Pop-Ups Within Pop-Ups

You may have realized already that you can cut pop-ups within your pop-ups. Try this form with the Basic Box Pop-Up first, since that one has the easiest folding and uses the same materials. Make sure you are working with a grain that cooperates with that fold.

1. Make a Basic Box Pop-Up (see page 12). Unfold.

2. Cut two wider slits above it and below it. Fold in the hinge between the wider slits in the same way, and then unfold.

3. Pop it. Push the larger box inside the tent.

4. Push the inner box back out through the smaller box. Close the whole thing and burnish. Open and close gently. You should have a box within a box.

This pop-up can work with any shape or combination, not just boxes. It's fun with semicircles. You can leave space for your hinges in different positions, with some higher and some lower on the circle. Then when you open it the motion gets interesting.

Always try these with scrap paper to work out kinks before you make something. Depending on the angles, the pop-ups can stick out the sides or top, so figure that out before you cut into nicer paper. Keep in mind that you can add a larger cover (covers are coming up soon—page 27!) to hide the works if you need to.

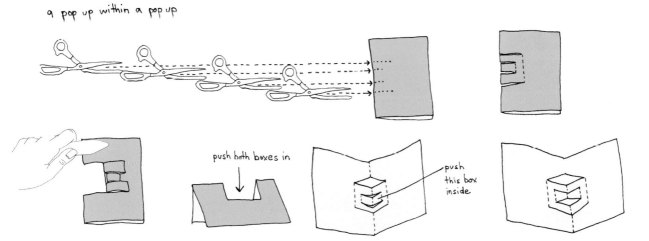

a pop up within a pop up

push both boxes in

push this box inside

Circle with Slits

I learned this interesting variation from Sue Kazoyan, who took my Artists' Books class at Cooper Union. Sue worked as a temp and would make things from the stuff she found in the desks where she worked as a receptionist for the day. She has since gone on to more career-oriented work, but in her temp days, she did not let her hands become the devil's plaything. Or maybe she did.

YOU WILL NEED
Basic pop-up materials (see page 8)
Empty cup or jar to use as a pattern
Ruler or triangle (optional)

1. Position the cup so that it's halfway over the fold.

2. Trace firmly around the edge of the glass with a pencil or your bone folder point, making a semicircle.

3. Cut straight across from the fold to the edge of the circle multiple times, making a series of parallel slices—an uneven number of slits works best. You can eyeball it or measure using a ruler. I recommend doing it fast to learn it. Cut both ends of the circle.

4. Fold each slit strip back so that it folds on the scored circle.

5. Burnish with your bone folder.

6. Open those folds, turn the pop-up over, fold back the other way, and burnish again.

7. Open the folds.

8. Open the base to make a tent.

9. Hold the tent steady and push the strips through.

10. Close the pop-up, burnish, then open and shut the card. Nice, huh?!

Variation

You can fold alternate strips. Trace the circle pattern lightly in pencil instead of using your bone folder. Cut your slits, but only score the ones you want to fold. Keep track with faint pencil lines. Erase later (use a gentle plastic eraser) if these lines show on your finished piece.

The alternating cuts look interesting from the outside, but you can add a cover (see page 27).

circle with slits

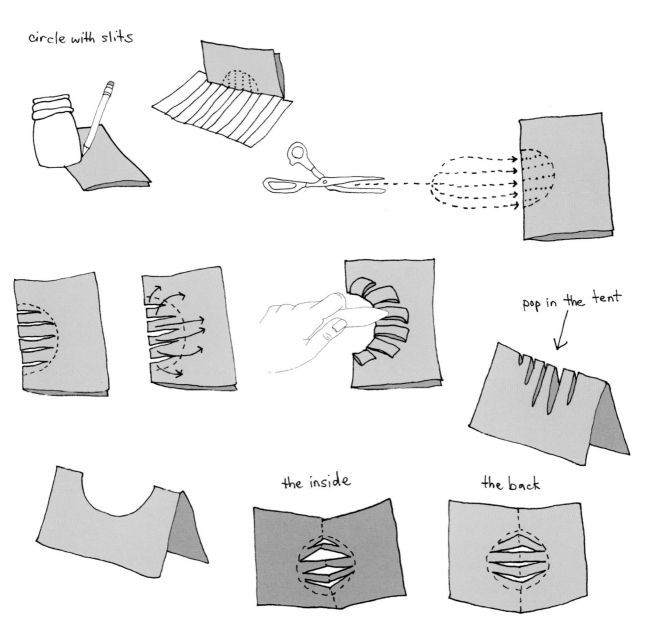

pop in the tent

the inside

the back

Tumbling Triangles

It's tricky. (Don't hurt yourself!)

I want to warn you about this one. Pop-ups didn't come easy for me, and I developed these Tumbling Triangles over a period of years, when my mind was ready to wrap around them, or break through the planes as necessary. If this is easy for you, you'll think I'm being ridiculous, and you probably won't understand how it can be hard for some people, but trust me, it is. If these other pop-ups have been tricky for you, don't try this one yet. Wait and practice until you have developed precision, can fold with verve, and are comfortable breaking through the paper plane.

OK. You're sure you want to do this?

Use the same materials you used for Pop-Up Basics (see page 8).

1. Cut a little slit at a 45-degree angle up into the pre-folded blank.

2. Fold at a 45-degree angle, finishing the triangle. Burnish like crazy. Open and fold in reverse and burnish like crazy again.

3. Pop it up, and then un pop it.

4. Now cut a slit parallel to (and a little longer than) the fold you just made.

5. Fold parallel to the first slit. Burnish like crazy again. Unfold.

6. Now cut a slit parallel to and even longer than the fold you just made (parallel to your original slit).

7. Fold parallel to your last slit. And burnish like crazy again. Open.

8. Make your tent—working from the larger triangle down, pop the biggest one in.

9. Pop the middle one out.

10. And pop the smallest one in.

11. Make sure they haven't made unintended folds. The paper really doesn't want to do this! When you are sure it's fine, gently open and close to check the action. Is it OK?

12. If it's OK, then burnish like crazy one more time.

13. Pat yourself on the back. Good work!

Don't you love the cool action of these tumbling triangles? I have one of these with a tumbling poem about motion.

Tumbling Triangles, EKS.

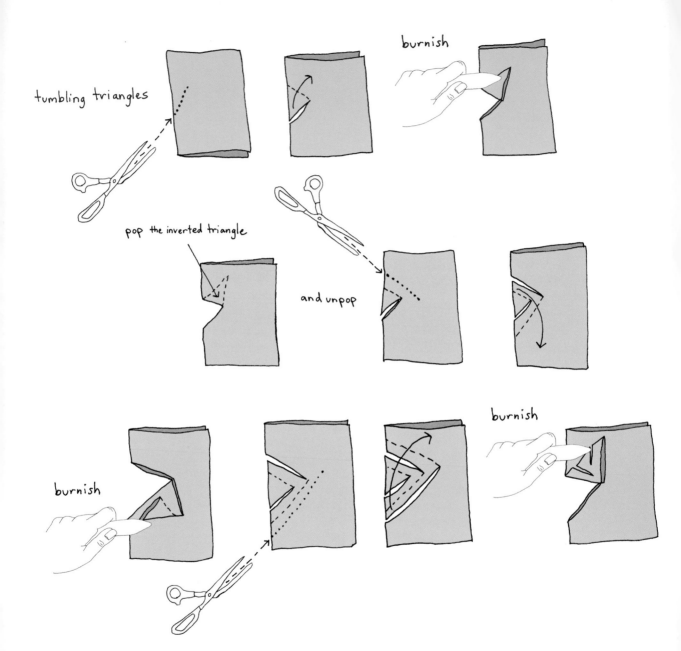

tumbling triangles

burnish

pop the inverted triangle

and unpop

burnish

burnish

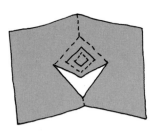 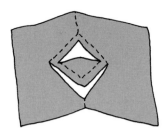 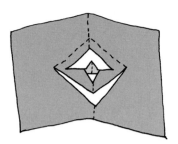

pop out the big triangle pop in the middle triangle pop out the smallest triangle

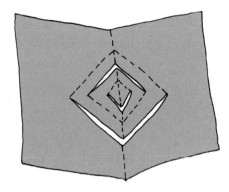 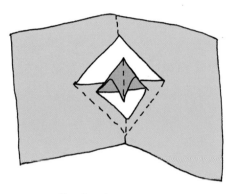

the inside unpopped the back open

Once you get these basic concepts, you can go further on your own. You know yourself. Are you super-precise? Do you like to measure? Do you like to work with X-Acto® knives? Tweezers? Toothpicks? Can you glue without making a mess?

The people I know who are really great at pop-ups taught themselves by taking apart pop-up books and cards. Make friends with your local kids' bookseller. The pop-up books on display don't last long. Your bookseller may be able to sell you the damaged ones really cheap.

Take them apart and learn from them. My daughter's kindergarten teacher had parents bring in broken small appliances for the kids to deconstruct—same thing! Or ask some kids to give you their hand-me-down messed-up pop-up books to take apart and play with.

There are lots of classes. And many books. I find books easy to understand, but everyone has their own learning style. Sometimes I'll look at a book and the pictures make sense, even if the written directions don't.

Pop-Up French Fold Card

I knew how to do this years before I knew it was called the French fold. When I was a kid, most greeting cards were printed on one side of thin paper and then folded in quarters. I'd take my dad's typing paper, fold it in half crosswise and then in half vertically, so it made its own cover. Then I would draw on it to make my own greeting cards. If I opened all the folds, the cover was upside down from the inside. Last year, my brother sent me a Halloween card he had sent me when I was three years old and he was in the Navy. Because it was a French fold, I was able to open it up, and color photocopy it. French fold is great for photocopying, because you don't need to worry about registering your printing on both sides.

If you want to do a French fold with thicker paper, pre-score with your bone folder and a straightedge. Double scores can be useful on even thicker paper. When you think about it (enlarge it in your mind): with a double score the paper folds only 90 degrees twice. That's much less stress on the paper fibers than a single 180 degree fold.

YOU WILL NEED

Thin paper—it's one-sided, so try it first with that 8½ x 11" (21.5 x 28cm) waste paper that you are recycling
Bone folder
Scissors

1. Fold your paper in half horizontally. Fold the paper in half vertically. See—it looks like a card with its own cover. Pencil lightly to indicate the cover and the inside, so you'll know it when you unfold it.

2. Open and fold vertically, reversing your interior vertical fold.

3. Cut and fold a simple pop-up on one half of the piece as shown.

4. Pop it (as you did for your samples, making the tent). Fold down the uncut piece for your cover to hide the works.

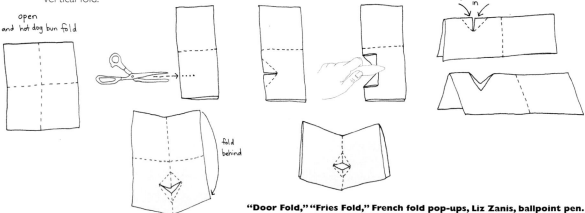

"Door Fold," "Fries Fold," French fold pop-ups, Liz Zanis, ballpoint pen.

Silly Photo Pop-Up Card

This is a small paper version of those simple amusement park attractions that you pose with to have your picture snapped. Your family hides behind space guys or giraffes or pirates and looks out through the holes, so their faces show in a funny scene—like a visual Mad Lib!

YOU WILL NEED

One Basic Box Pop-Up French Fold Card (see page 20)
Adhesive
One portrait (school photos are nice)
Cover paper
Scissors

1. Adhere the photo to the small box pop-up (see page 12).

2. Carefully mark where the photo sits when the pop-up is closed.

3. Cut a hole in the pop-up paper so the face from the photo is visible.

4. You can draw around the face on the cover. When I did this with my daughter Georgia's fourth-grade picture, I drew a princess on the outer cover. When you opened the card, she popped up in her school clothes.

You can use store-bought envelopes to send your cards. If you do, buy them first and make your cards to match, or at least know their measurements. Allow some space around the outside of the card. Your card should be at least ½" (1.3cm) smaller than your envelope to allow for paper thickness and layers. It's a choice you make for yourself. I have had some clients who like very tight envelopes and others who prefer more space. Both think their way is correct. Embellish your pop-ups with drawings, collage, rubber stamps, or even glitter pens or glue with glitter (allow time for it to dry!). Use whatever seems like fun. Or supply a child with some markers and pop-ups for drawing. These make great one-of-a-kind birthday or get-well cards.

a silly pop up card

a school picture

a basic pop up

trace where the face
will be when the cover
is closed.

Pop-Up Instant Book

If you don't know how to make an instant book, here's a quick lesson.

YOU WILL NEED

8½ x 11" (21.5 x 28cm) recycled office paper, or anything you can fold—larger or smaller rectangle or square is OK
Bone folder
Scissors

1. Fold the paper lengthwise, burnish with a bone folder, and open.

2. Lightly fold the paper horizontally. Don't burnish this fold until the little book is finished.

3. Fold the two open ends up to the middle, front and back, and burnish. Then open those folds partway.

4. Cut a slit in the center on the vertical fold line from the center fold down to the interior fold as shown.

5. Grasp the horizontal middle fold on both sides of the slit, and pull apart and down.

6. Push into a book form, finagling as necessary. Voilà!

7. To make this into a pop-up, take a good look at the form. You have several valley folds that will work for pop-ups. Don't cut the front or back cover. If you make pop-ups in all three spreads, the works show, so they need to relate to each other, like squares growing larger, or be the same exact shape. It is safest to make a pop-up either in the first and last spreads, or only in the middle. To do this, you need to turn your book inside out, cut and fold your pop-up, and then turn the book right-side out again. My brain hurts as I write this. It's not difficult so much as sort of confusing. Mark the spreads lightly in pencil to keep things straight. Try it out on recycled paper, and when you get the hang of it, do it for real. Cut a basic, one-fold pop-up in the center to start and go from there.

Note: Multiple pop-ups can get pretty thick with all the layers of paper, but you can allow more room for them. When you lightly fold the second (horizontal) fold, instead of having the edges match, leave a little margin, ¼" (0.64cm) or so. This allows one side to be bigger for the cover. You need to experiment with this to get it right.

Remember: Make dummies and try things in various sketch versions and then make a finished piece based on what you develop with this process. Some dummies are for planning the book, others, binding dummies, are to make sure the structure works with the thickness of your paper. If you are planning to use a really expensive paper, first experiment with something cheaper that is similar in weight and texture. Warning: Inkjet papers have a coating that can crack when folded. One friend planned a whole edition that was all printed and then didn't work because of that problem. Carpenters say, "Measure twice, cut once." Time spent planning an edition saves frustration (and time and $$!) later.

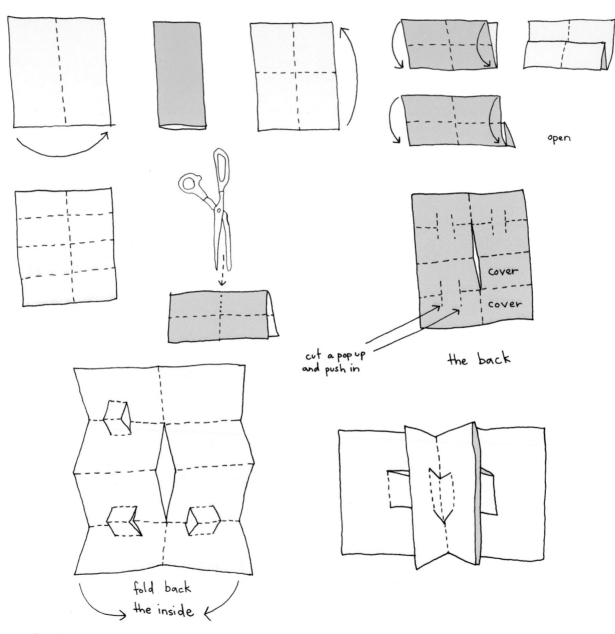

open

cut a pop up
and push in

cover

cover

the back

fold back
the inside

Pop! 26

Adding a Cover

There are several ways to add a cover. I'll show you the easiest first, though it does involve adhesive. A glue stick is fine for learning this technique. Double-stick tape or brushed-on paste may be your preference if you go into production, making holiday cards or invitations. At least one of my Cooper Union students started a handmade card company. Choose cover papers that are heavy enough to stand, but light enough to fold—heavyweight, 90-pound cover paper works well. You can use thinner paper if you are adding a cover or making a self cover via French fold (see page 20). Experiment and design around your papers.

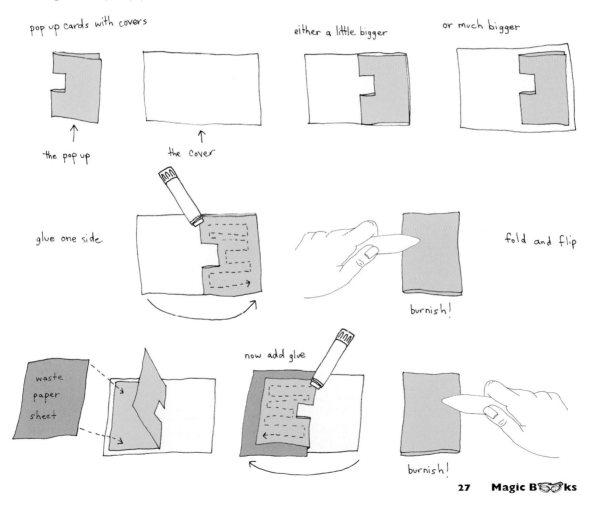

pop up cards with covers

either a little bigger

or much bigger

the pop up

the cover

glue one side.

burnish!

fold and flip

waste paper sheet

now add glue

burnish!

Spring Equinox March 20, 1994

Pop-Up Accordion

YOU WILL NEED

A long short-grain piece of heavy, foldable paper
Bone folder
Scissors

1. Fold an accordion.

2. Cut and fold simple pop-ups on the mountains and/or valleys, leaving the first and last folds uncut.

3. Add covers if you like. There are many ways to do covers—I'll refer you to my first book, *How to Make Books*, for info on this, but basically, you can adhere raw board or covered board to each end, or fold a flat back cover from heavy but foldable paper and attach your accordion at the front, back, or spine if your accordion has a little paper left over.

4. Keep everything flush at the bottom so your pop-up accordion can stand. You can cut the top edge into shapes if you like.

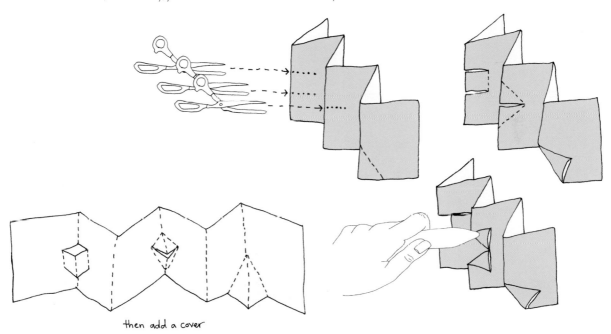

then add a cover

"Fallen from My Bag," Liz Zanis, Inkjet pop-up. Right: "Spring has Sproing,"
Purgatory Pie Press die-cut and hand-set type, letterpress on handmade paper
with watermark by Helen Hiebert, Dieu Donne.

flip!

Flip books are fun! The Museum of the Moving Image in Astoria, New York, where motion pictures began, has fascinating examples of pre-movie moving pictures, including flip books and other early animation inventions and machines. In a soundstage setup you can jump around (or kiss your sweetie) and have a flip book photographed that you can later buy for a few dollars in their gift shop.

"Contraption Device," Purgatory Pie Press artist proof, letterpress from antique engravings.

31   Magic Books

Pocket Movies

For the binding you will need to choose the method that works best for you. You can staple if you have access to a heavy-duty stapler. You will need to cover the staples, though, so they don't pierce your hand. Bookbinding tape works for this. Or make a cuff with more of your paper and glue it on. Pound staple ends in with a mallet before you cover them. Or glue your pages together like Post-It® pads with a glue stick or double-stick tape. Or drill and sew with linen thread, or tie with ribbon. You can even use paper bolts from a bookbinding supplier or stationery store.

YOU WILL NEED
Short-grain cover stock, or use a Post-It pad, tablet corner, or 3 x 5" (7.6 x 12.7cm) cards
Pen and ink, or markers
Binding materials

1. Cut your paper. Be precise or have someone cut it for you on a guillotine—some copy shops can do that. You can also work with precut cards, unlined (or even lined) index cards, or playing cards (imagine collaging on them!).

2. Keep your main shape low on the page. (Only the bottom third to a quarter of the page shows when you flip the book.) Sketch your pocket movie idea lightly in pencil and try it out. There are various ways to do this. You can make an animation, something doing something. Or use a photocopy machine, shrinking a picture (or text) smaller and smaller and smaller until it disappears, or enlarging and enlarging the enlargement forever. Holly Anderson and Janet Zweig made their artist book *She-herezade* (Pyramid Atlantic, 1988) with each of 5 stories growing larger page by page from a single letter from the previous story.

Changing patterns can be interesting to work with, or colors fading into the next color. One way to do this is to sketch the same simple shape in the same place on every page, and changing the color intensity. (I'm writing in an Ellsworth Kelly room at MoMA, so I'm inspired by his odd and simple shapes—say, a rounded triangle or a rectangle with one curved side.)

"Okay Day," Liz Zanis, screenprint flip book.

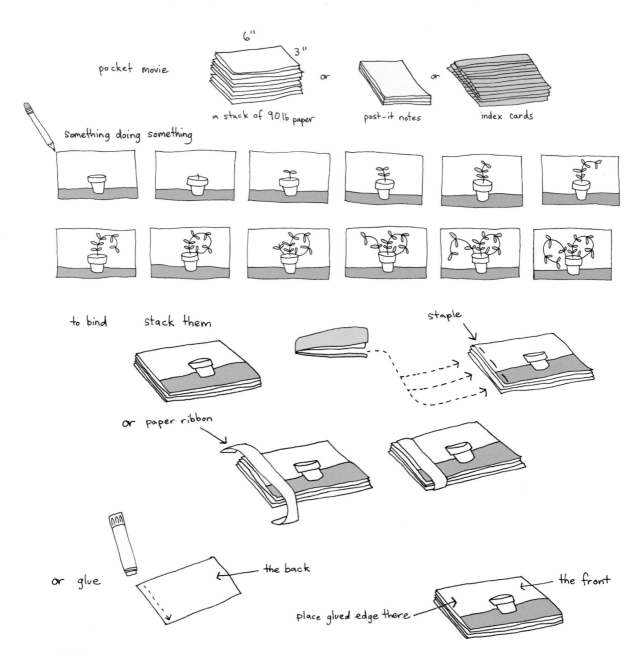

pocket movie

6" 3"

a stack of 90 lb paper   post-it notes   index cards

or   or

Something doing something

to bind   stack them

staple

or paper ribbon

or glue   the back

place glued edge there   the front

Stab Binding

The simple stab stitch is often called Japanese binding. The thing is, there are other Japanese bindings and this stitch is also common in China, Korea, and Thailand. You will need a blunt, large-holed darning needle and linen thread.

1. Drill or punch two holes. Take a blunt large holed darning needle and a length of linen thread.

2. Start with one end hole. Pull your thread in, leaving a tail on the back that is long enough to tie later.

3. Wrap the thread around the spine and come back through the same hole.

4. Wrap around the top (or bottom) and come back again through the same hole.

5. Go to your next hole. Wrap around the spine and back through the same hole.

6. If this is your last hole, wrap the thread around the bottom (or top). If this is not your last hole, keep going through the holes, wrapping the spine at every hole till you get to the end, and then wrap the thread around the end.

7. Now come back through the hole (or holes), filling in the blank spaces. Tie off with a square knot when you get to the final hole (which may have happened right after step 6).

8. You can leave your thread ends long, attach buttons or beads (or bells or whistles) to them, or try to work them into the interior of the book.

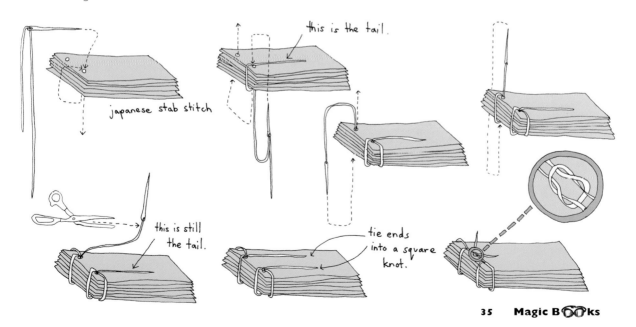

this is the tail.

japanese stab stitch

this is still the tail.

tie ends into a square knot.

Flip Book with Eraser Stamps

An easy idea is to carve a simple bird shape and have it fly around your flip book. Or an abstract shape can move around the pages.

YOU WILL NEED

Paper

Soft marker

Smooth plastic erasers, like Stabilo

X-Acto® knife with sharp blades, or scalpel, and/or linoleum carving tools

Stamp pads

or printer's ink (water base is easier to clean up), hand rollers, and plate glass or Plexiglas to roll out your ink

1. Plan your picture on paper if you like.

2. Draw with a soft marker onto the eraser (don't scratch the surface—that would show up when you stamp it later).

3. Carve. Be careful. A hardware glove for your non-carving hand can help protect you. It's important to set yourself up on a good work surface. Sweep that clutter onto the floor, and make sure you have good light and a seat that gives you the right angle for carving. Don't work with sharp tools when you are tired.

4. Stamp with a stamp pad, or if you want to get fancy, roll out the printmaking inks on a piece of Plexiglas and ink and print your tiny eraser stamp. Artist Sage Coleman made multicolored eraser stamp prints. This doesn't go with my more-bang-for-the-buck philosophy, but the results were really beautiful. If you have the fine motor skills, time, and energy, go for it. There are all kinds of cool products in the rubber-stamp world, including powders you can brush on for special effect.

You don't need to use rubber stamps only for flip books. Many of these projects would be great with rubber-stamp embellishments. I worked with a group at the NY Art Book Fair on an instant publishing project. We made white paper instant books, stamped them with a cool collection of rubber stamps, and then photocopied them onto various papers.

You could also use a rubber-stamp alphabet, and stamp a word or your name and have it move or change.

Try this project with collage. If the images are black and white, you can photocopy them to enlarge or make into an edition. If they are color, you could scan and print or color photocopy.

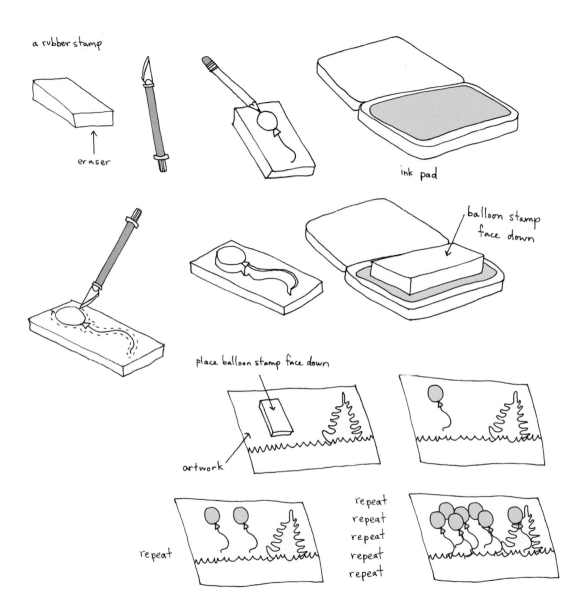

a rubber stamp

eraser

ink pad

balloon stamp
face down

place balloon stamp face down

artwork

repeat

repeat
repeat
repeat
repeat
repeat

FOLD!

Folding is practical magic—it turns two dimensions into three. Take a sheet of paper, fold it in half, and you have 4 pages. Folding almost seems like nothing! But it's crucial. A student who was otherwise astute in so many ways, asked, after you know how to do this, you don't have to fold, do you? Yes, you do. But a good fold is easy when you slow down and treat it with the respect it deserves. And folding well gets faster with repetition and becomes second nature. Just never forget to fold with verve!

"Red, Yellow, Blue," Alice Austin, offset lithography, map fold.

Origami Star Book

If you already have experience with origami, these projects will be very easy. When I was in high school, I carried a pocket candy tin with tiny squares of crisp typing paper that I'd fold into miniature cranes when I was bored in class—I hadn't heard that "Thousand Cranes" story, but I folded at least that many. When I first saw these origami books, I immediately "got" them—it didn't occur to me that someone had invented them, but it turns out that San Francisco artist Anna Wolf is credited with this form.

This can be a book or an ornament. It folds flat, so you can mail it in an envelope as a card that—voilà!—is also a gift. You can even cut some simple pop-ups (see Pop!, page 6) into the folds.

YOU WILL NEED

3 or 4 squares of paper—foil wrapping paper is nice for Star Book ornaments
Bone folder
Adhesive
Card stock for cover (optional)
Heavy thread, thin string, or ribbon for cover (optional)

Base

1. Fold a square on the diagonal. Open, and turn the paper over. Make a horizontal and vertical fold. Pinch the folded corners and push together. The diagonal fold will engage and you will have a diamond/square.

2. Notice how one point is the center of all the folds, the opposite point is where all corners come together, and the other two side points contain the diagonal.

Star Book

1. Make three or four of these bases (above). Or more if you can't stop.

2. Adhere three bases together, putting your adhesive on the flat outside of the base, so that the closed points all match up. Burnish well with your bone folder.

3. Let the adhesive dry. If it feels cool when you touch it, it's not dry. Paper adhered with wet glue or paste needs to dry under weight, changing waste sheets to wick away the moisture. Glue-stick glue needs to dry only for a short time. Double-stick tape does not.

4. When fully dry, open the bases gently and hold the outer sides together. Look at this shape, and see how you like it. It's simple, but interesting. You can stop with three if you like, or add a fourth for a fuller, more flowery shape. You can even add a fifth base if you want a fuller shape.

"Grass Sample Origami Star," Liz Zanis, screenprint with screenprinted balsa wood covers.

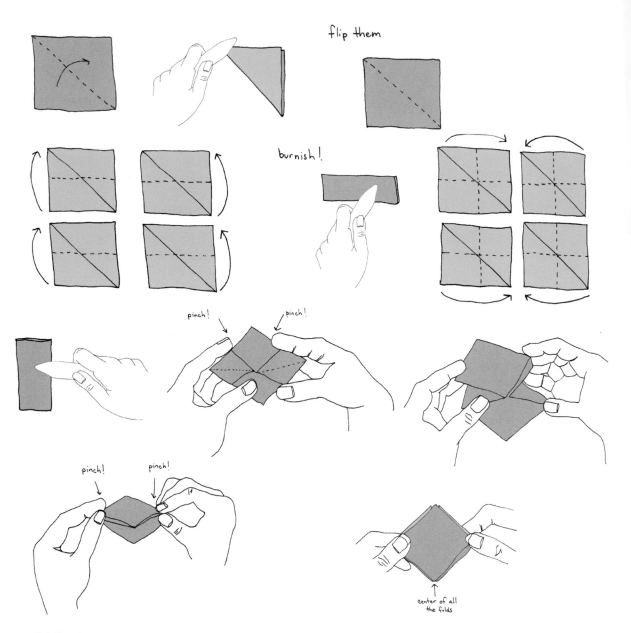

flip them

burnish!

pinch!   pinch!

pinch!   pinch!

center of all
the folds

Now if you just want to hang this or make an ornament, you could glue the outer ends together. But I call this a book. And now we get into philosophy—*What is a book?* There are conferences on this. People present for hours, for days, for weeks, for years and years—there are Web groups devoted to this, about "in the page" and "on the page." My eyelids are drooping—need coffee-e-e-e-e-e.

I will say that one way to differentiate a book from, say, an ornament or paper sculpture is that it can open and close. It's a transformer. And it's easy to store. I sometimes think I got into making books because I lived in a very small apartment when I moved to New York City. Ruth and Marvin Sackner, who may have the most extensive collection of artists' books in the world, told me that they started collecting books when they ran out of wall space for paintings.

Star Book Cover

The simplest cover—and for this quick model, you should go simple—is this one:

1. Cut two pieces of card stock the size of your folded square.

2. Cut a piece of heavy thread or thin string or ribbon long enough to go around the book on the diagonal, and then tie.

3. Adhere the thread/ribbon/string/tie to the outside pages as shown.

4. Adhere the square card pieces over the thread, burnish, and let dry or settle.

5. Then, gently open your book and tie it open—voilà!

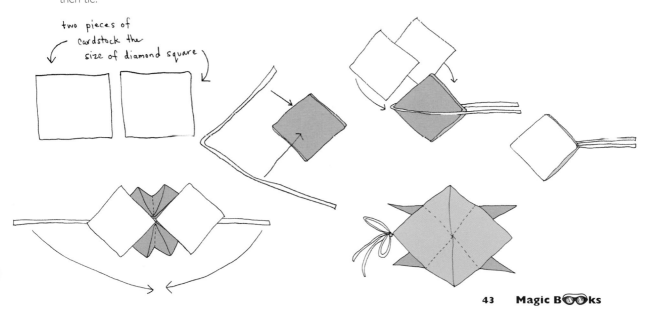

two pieces of cardstock the size of diamond square

Snake Book

Snake books start with the same base as star books, but you put them together the opposite way. And they can go on indefinitely. They are great for group projects, party ice breakers, and gifts for those pesky people who have everything.

YOU WILL NEED
Square pieces of paper folded into origami bases—5 or more
Bone folder
Adhesive of choice
Cover materials (see page 41)

1. Adhere so the opposite corners meet up. I use my hands to demonstrate this. For the Origami Star Book (page 41), place your hands, palm together (like a clap). And keeping the bottom of your palm together, open them so that the fingers go apart. That is how the star version works. For the Snake Book, place your hands together, fingers to palm and palm to fingers—this is the placement for the snake book. Alternate as you go.

2. Burnish and let dry.

3. Gently open—it grows to a long banner, or book.

Snake Book Cover

You can make simple covers with ribbons (similar to the Star Book Cover on page 43), but have the ribbon ends come out both sides. Use two ribbons instead of one long one, so that the ribbons can tie shut in two places.

burnish!

3rd diamond square

4th diamond square

4th diamond square

5th diamond square

"Coffee," Alice Austin, snakebook of linoleum cuts on stonehenge paper, with painted book board covers.

Pop-Up Map Fold

You may have seen these in those New York Popout and Paris Popout maps. I remember getting one just because it was so cute. This isn't exactly the same, but it's very close. It pops up with great, surprising motion, so makes sense for other things, not just maps. Our favorite project, for when you've learned to fold this, is a surprise party invitation (see page 50). We made these for David Letterman's mother when she celebrated her eighty-fifth birthday.

YOU WILL NEED

Lightweight rectangular paper
Cover stock
Adhesive
Bone folder

1. Fold in half vertically, then open.

2. Fold the paper in half horizontally. Open and reverse to fold the other way. This fold prepares the paper to turn inside out when it pops up. Have the fold at the bottom and the open ends at the top.

3. Bring the bottom corners into the middle so that folded edges meet and there is a point at the bottom as shown. Burnish, reverse folds, burnish again.

4. Push those folds to the inside: Pinch one side, unfold the opposite corner, open the edge, and tuck what had been the bottom fold into the center. It sort of pops in if you've folded it well, when you open that side.

Repeat this on the other side. In origami, this is sometimes called a squash fold. It's the trickiest part of this map fold.

5. Now fold the short flat sides into the center of the paper, both on the front and the back. Burnish well, and reverse the folds in both directions.

6. Just as you did in step 6, tuck these folds into the inside. Unfold, put your forefinger inside, and push in with your thumb. Repeat this with all four folds, as shown. Burnish.

7. Try opening and closing it—it should pop open and refold.

"The Secret," Susan Happersett, pop-up map fold surprise party invitation, color photocopied collage.

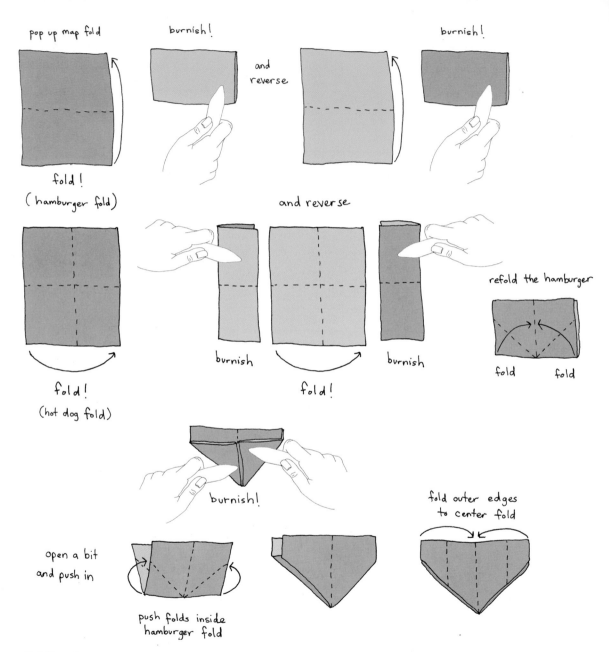

pop up map fold

burnish!

and reverse

burnish!

fold!
(hamburger fold)

and reverse

burnish

fold!
(hot dog fold)

burnish

refold the hamburger

fold   fold

burnish!

open a bit
and push in

push folds inside
hamburger fold

fold outer edges
to center fold

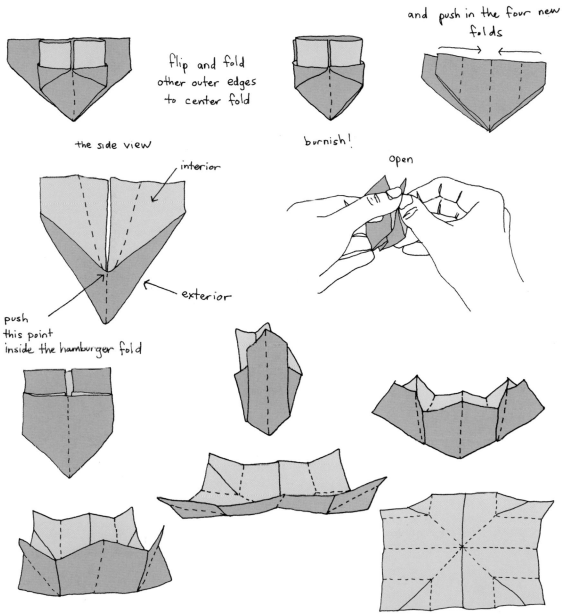

flip and fold
other outer edges
to center fold

and push in the four new
folds

burnish!

the side view

interior

exterior

open

push
this point
inside the hamburger fold

Pop-Up Map Cover

1. Cut a piece of cover paper a little wider than your folded lightweight piece and a little more than twice as long.

2. Fold it in half horizontally to make a cover.

3. Place the map fold inside, with the point almost touching the fold of the cover.

4. Put adhesive onto the inside lightweight paper, fold the cover up, and close it over the inner piece.

5. Burnish the cover over the adhesive.

6. Turn the piece over, open the other side, put adhesive on the inner folded paper, and close the cover on that side.

Doing it this way, opening and closing the cover, might seem odd, but it allows for the right amount of hinging space, so that the piece will open without ripping the paper.

Try this a few times with junk paper until you get the hang of it.

Now you can make Surprise Party Invitations!

Surprise Party Invitations!

The Pop-Up Map makes a great party invitation. If making your invitations on black-and-white photocopy, make your map fold from lightweight white paper. Draw with black pens, soft pencils, or black markers. Sharpies® work, but I hate their toxic smell, so use a water-based version. As long as you don't cry on it, the invitation doesn't need to be waterproof.

Note: You can fold photocopies or printouts with this method, but try a few before you commit to them. Sometimes toner will rub off if it's on the fold. As much as possible, design your interior so that there is no printing on the fold. Drawing with markers should not be a problem, but caution is the better part of valor. Or as I always say: Experiment as you go!

If you would like to add collage elements, like a baby picture of the honored guest, use black-and-white photos and images from black-and-white sources. Try anything you would like to put on your collage on a photocopy and see how it looks. It can be interesting to photocopy all kinds of objects: fortune cookie fortunes, jewelry, the contents of your pockets, flowers, etc. Experiment with this stuff, and design around it.

For the type on your invitation you could cut words and letters from magazines ransom-note style or write or print it in a neat or interesting way.

I want to caution you about calligraphy. When it isn't done well, it's really bad. Please keep your writing unpretentious. If you want to use calligraphy, learn how, or have a real calligrapher do it. This piece is sort of silly, so I recommend keeping it light. A little kid could write the words. Or you could hire teenybopper girls who are into their handwriting and dot their i's with happy faces, daisies, and hearts. I like hiring those girls to address envelopes, too, and they can always use the $$! Other people whose handwriting can be lovely are older ladies who were taught penmanship in school. People who don't use computers sometimes have very nice handwriting. As you may know, Andy Warhol used his mother's handwriting for his early illustration work.

So mess around, design your invitation, and when it's time to print, you do not need to print onto white paper. You can use any color that looks good with black ink.

If you have access to a color photocopier (my daughter's computer came with a free printer/scanner—the ink isn't free, of course!), your original can be any colors you like. It's nice to make your original in color on white paper. Print onto color paper so that the background color is in the paper, not in the ink. Then it's less likely to crack when you fold it. But of course experiment with printing and folding one before you get too far into it.

Invitation Covers

If the cover-weight paper will feed through the photocopier, great. Otherwise, you can photocopy onto sticky-back paper and make a label, or photocopy onto regular lightweight paper and adhere. Sheets of double-stick tape can be very handy for this sort of thing. If you set up your originals to copy several labels at a time and back the whole sheet with double-stick tape, then you can just cut up and adhere all at once—this isn't worth the trouble for five or ten, but if you are making twenty-five or more it saves time and materials. It's also good to know this technique for future publishing projects.

Making stickers is also useful when you want to use color images without spending the money for color copies. Put as many pictures as you can onto your original, and then chop it up and use for a touch of color on cheaper copies.

Obviously, much of this can be done via Photoshop on the computer if you know how. Though (as artist Stephanie Brody-Lederman always reminds me) the mark of the hand can be most beautiful.

Shaped Pamphlet

You can make a pamphlet book in any shape that you like, within reason. You just need a tall enough spine to support the book. The bigger the spine, the more stable the book. Of course, some books don't need to be very sturdy. I design a date book every year, so I am always trying to make something that will last through rough, everyday, throw-in-your pocket, spill-things-on-it, leaky pen use. But many books are enjoyed occasionally. Think about what the book's function is when you design its structure. Some are gifts that will be treasured, but not abused. Anything made for children should be designed for rough use. But ephemera is also nice. Not everything should last forever. Imagine how cluttered the world would be if it did. When my kids were little, I used to wish that cheap plastic toys had a half-life and would fade away if no one played with them for a week or so.

YOU WILL NEED

Paper to play with

Scissors

Text-weight paper, enough for 4 to 8 folded sheets, depending on thickness

Endsheet paper (optional)

Cover-weight paper

X-Acto® knife, plus cutting mat and sharp scissors

Linen thread

Awl

Needle

1. Try out shapes with scissors and a single sheet of folded paper. Cut shapes that look interesting when open or closed.

2. When you decide on a shape, cut thin paper for the pages and end sheets, if you want them, and heavier paper for the covers. Keep in mind that as you fold a few sheets of paper, the paper thickness adds up bit by bit, so the outside sheet needs to be a little larger than the inside. This is not necessarily a problem, just something to be aware of. You can use a knife and cut a folded section all at the same time, or cut with scissors, making each page a tiny bit larger than the last, or not worry about it, if a slight edge showing doesn't bother you.

3. Make the covers just a bit larger than the inside. You can fold the inside sheets and trace the cover around them to be sure there is enough room. How much extra is up to you. Some people like a very even ⅛" (0.32cm), but it's an arbitrary decision. Sometimes I make a much larger cover than the inside.

"Larry Thoughts," Liz Zanis, shaped pamphlet; antique children's apple book.

When I'm designing these fun little books, I try to get into an improvisational mode, play with my papers, try a few things, and go with what feels right. If you believe in left brain/right brain (I heard on NPR that researchers have now discovered many more sides to the brain), that is a good way to approach this. Let your right brain play with ideas and try things out. When it comes up with a cool idea, let your left brain take over and do the math and solve the practical problems.

4. Stitch with the three-hole pamphlet stitch as per the illustration. With your awl, pierce three holes through the spine of the text pages, end sheets, and cover: one in the middle, one above, and one below. Keep the top and bottom ones more than ½" (1.3cm) from the edges. Note: You can aso punch holes and sew with a ribbon.

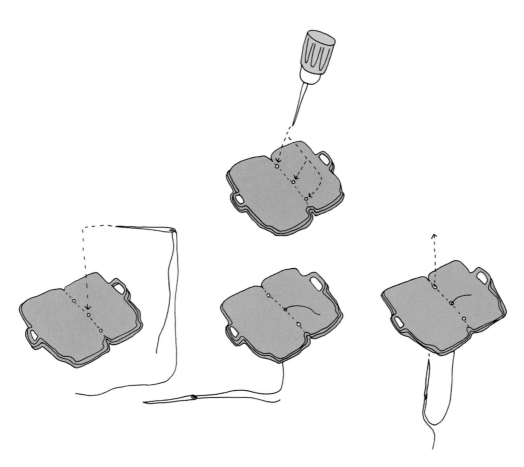

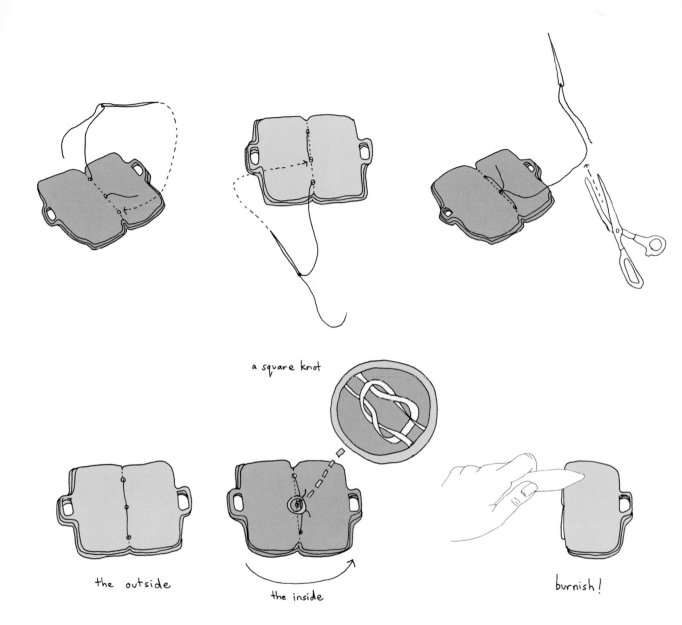

a square knot

the outside

the inside

burnish!

Jogged Pamphlet

This is another one of my favorite bang-for-your-buck formats. This is an easy way to make something interesting-looking—I've found examples in menus, cookbooks, vintage appliance instructions. Since the pages don't line up, hints are revealed of what's to come.

YOU WILL NEED

Four pieces of paper in two contrasting colors
Bone folder
Needle
Thread
Awl

1. Lay one sheet of paper horizontally.

2. Alternating colors, line your paper up flush at the bottom, but jogged ¾" (2cm) or so on the left side, so that you see stripes of the alternating colors.

3. Fold the sheaf of paper so that the innermost sheet folds exactly in half, and the other sheets line up in stripes on both sides.

4. Before you crease, make sure that the stripes are the right size—they may need to be adjusted closer together for this to work. When you are happy with the arrangement, crease and burnish.

5. Stitch with a three-hole pamphlet stitch (see page 54).

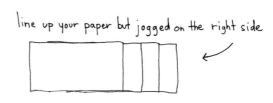

line up your paper but jogged on the right side

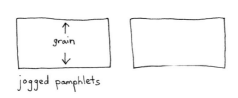

grain

jogged pamphlets

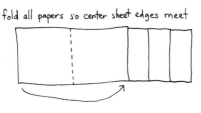

fold all papers so center sheet edges meet

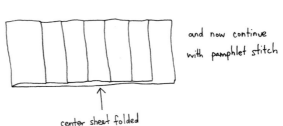

and now continue with pamphlet stitch

center sheet folded on itself

"Weeded Subway," Liz Zanis, jogged pamphlet. Found vintage instructional pamphlets

Pop-Up Pamphlet

Try this quickly with your one-sided office paper—make your French fold pop-up in one piece and use the other piece for your outer pages. There's no need to add a cover or endpapers; just try it.

YOU WILL NEED
Unsewn pamphlet book with endsheets and cover
French-fold pop-up folded to the same size as a page of the pamphlet (instructions on page 20)
Scissors
Linen thread
Dull needle
Awl

1. Fold a French fold the same size as your page spread

2. Cut your pop-up, pop it, burnish, and check it. Unfold and re- fold vertically.

3. Line up French fold bottom with your outer pages.

4. Stitch (see pages 54-55) the uncut end of the French fold into the center spread with your other pages, endpapers and cover.

5. Fold down French fold, re-pop it and voilà!

Did you ever think it would be this easy to make your own pop up book? Now make it into something interesting.

Pop-up pamphlet, EKS, die-cut papers.

Cross-Stitch Star Book

A client came to the studio to propose a Golda Meir book with text from people who had known her. Among the various ideas was a six-pointed star cut out folded in half. It didn't look good, but in a flash of inspiration, I quickly grabbed a cut-off end of a beautiful thick white paper, folded twelve equilateral triangles, and cross-stitched them together into a tiny 3-D star. She presented it to the funders, and they said YES! I was credited as the book's "inventor." Among the Golda stories was one about how much she loved Häagen-Dazs. She had once stopped a plane on the tarmac to bring back a case of ice cream—I can totally relate to that!

YOU WILL NEED

Lightweight sheets of paper
Heavyweight paper for the covers (or boards, covered with cloth or paper if you like)
Scissors, or an X-Acto® knife and a straightedge
Triangle, protractor, or compass (optional)
Awl
Blunt darning needle
Linen thread

1. Cut the paper into at least 10 equilateral triangles (60°/60°/60°). A plastic or metal triangle, protractor, or compass can help with this.

2. Fold the triangles in half.

3. Arrange two folded triangles in opposite directions so they form a star. With the awl, pierce four sewing holes where the triangles intersect—one near the top, one near the bottom just up from where the triangles intersect (but not too close, where it would be likely to tear through the edge), and two closer to the middle. These triangles are your "mother" signature. Mark them lightly with pencil to indicate which is the top and which is the bottom.

4. Use the mother signature as a template to pierce the sewing holes in the other triangles. Punch holes in half of them to match the top triangle and the other half to match the bottom triangle.

5. Set up the triangles in a series of stars with the holes aligned.

6. Stitch, starting at the outside. Stitch the first signature star set in, out, in, out as shown. Add your next signature, matching the bottom holes, and stitch it to the first as shown.

"Almost Wooden,"Liz Zanis, screenprint cross-stitched star book.

7. At this point, adjust your tension, being careful not to rip through the paper, and tie a square knot: left over right and right over left. You will later thread that tail with a needle and sew it back into the book, so make it long.

8. Add your next signature, sewing in the top hole, out the next hole, and through the long center stitch, continuing your cross stitch, and out the bottom, as shown.

9. Go back with your thread and sew through that stitch at the bottom of your first two signatures, and then sew into the bottom hole of your next signature.

10. Continue in this same pattern: sew in, then out, picking up your big stitch from the previous center, back into your next hole, and out the top, as shown. Sew through the stitch between the previous two signatures and pick up the next signature.

11. When all your signatures have been stitched in this fashion, have your final stitch go through the stitch of the previous two signatures and then (unless you want to stitch on covers) come back in your final hole.

12. Tie off your thread by looping through your previous stitch and bringing your thread through that loop. Do this twice, and trim your thread. This is sometimes called a kettle stitch, but I think of it like the knot you make when you finish hand sewing, hemming, etc. (do people still hem?).

13. Go back to that first long tail, thread it onto your needle, and sew it into the signature. You can tie it off as you did for the final stitch and trim.

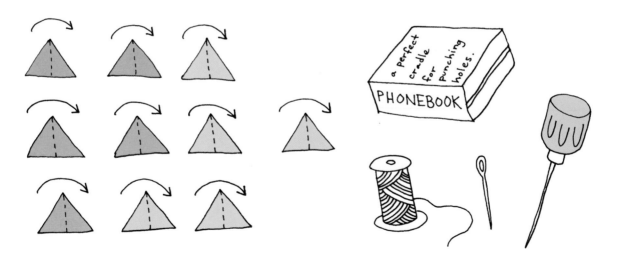

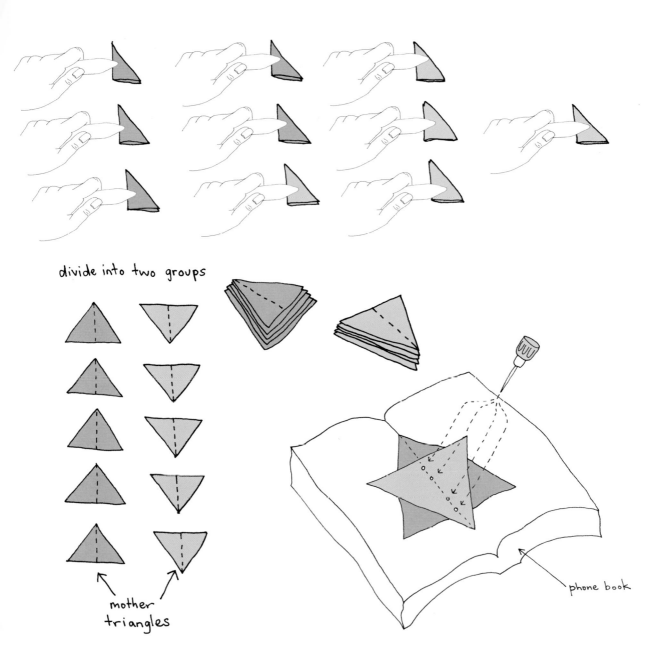

divide into two groups

mother triangles

phone book

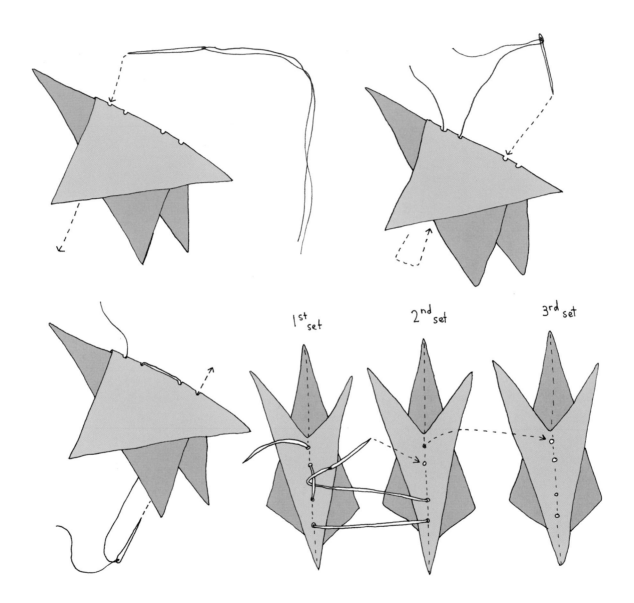

1st set   2nd set   3rd set

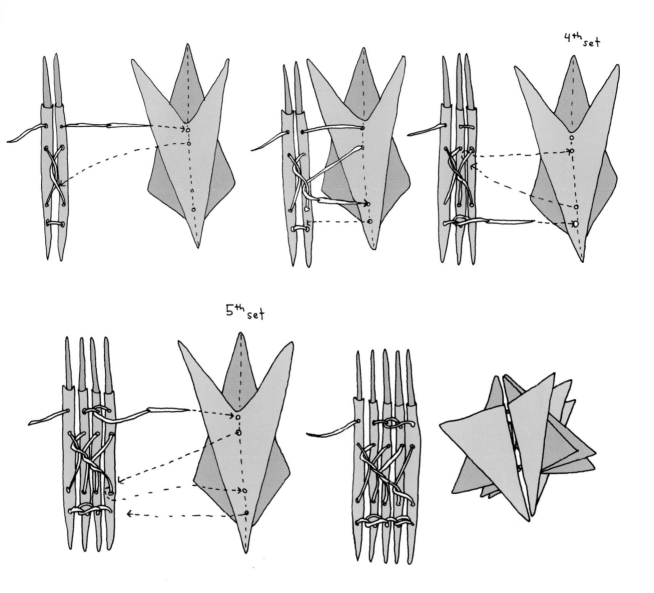

5th set

Accordion Flip-Flaps

Hedi Kyle, a well-known, inventive bookbinder, taught this form to many people who showed it to many other people. She doesn't claim to have invented it, but says she discovered it in her work restoring albums in medical and botanic libraries. I think of it as a flip-flap, because its action is interesting. And it can make a great sound. These flip-flaps are very easy—one of those bang-for-your-buck book forms. We used it to make a photo album with envelopes for notes as a gift of appreciation for some people who already had everything.

YOU WILL NEED
Heavy, foldable cover-weight paper (approximately 90-pound)
Heavy card stock, or actual cards
Bone folder
Scissors or utility knife and straightedge
Adhesive

1. Fold a narrow accordion from the cover-weight paper as shown. You can make this whatever size you like—but to learn it, make about eight folds. Make the height of the accordion at least 8" (20cm).

2. Cut heavy card stock into 2 x 4" (5 x 10cm) cards. Make twelve cards if your accordion has four mountain folds.

3. Lay three cards on alternating sides of one of the mountain folds so that they have about 1" (2.5cm) between them, with the 2" (5cm) side attached and the 4" (10cm) extending out.

4. Adhere the cards to the accordion and burnish well. Let dry if necessary.

5. Line up the rest of the cards so that they match on the other accordion folds and are adhered to the similar sides of the folds. Use the numbered diagram as a guide.

6. Adhere, burnish, and let dry.

7. When gently opened, the cards should flap in both directions without bumping. This can make a great photo album or guest book—or both! You could make one from business cards. That's a good way to try it out. Or use Band-Aids for a cool, floppy effect. Try using playing cards or baseball cards. I've made them from SAT-prep vocabulary cards.

"A 90th Birthday Party Powerpoint Flapbook," Liz Zanis, accordian flip-flap book. Inkjet print.

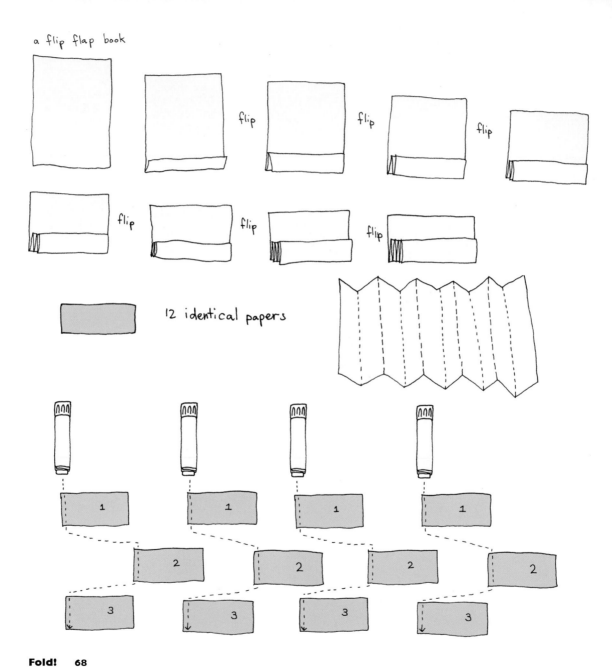

a flip flap book

flip

flip

flip

flip

flip

flip

12 identical papers

1

1

1

1

2

2

2

2

3

3

3

3

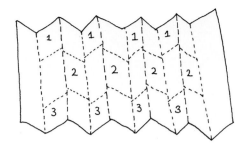

match the numbers with alternating sides of the mountain folds.

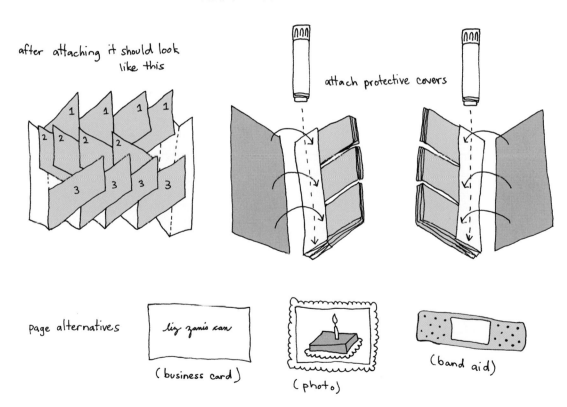

after attaching it should look like this

attach protective covers

page alternatives

liz zamis san

(business card)

(photo)

(band aid)

Self-Cover Flip-Flap

Use a long strip of heavyweight paper.

1. Fold the paper in half.

2. Decide on your cover dimension and fold the end back to that size. Match that fold on the other side.

3. Accordion-fold the middle section in half and in half again, reversing folds as necessary until you have a narrow accordion surrounded by covers.

4. Then cut, arrange, and adhere your cards (see page 66).

5. If the self-cover isn't sturdy enough, you can always adhere another layer. Or wrap another folded piece of card stock around each cover and adhere.

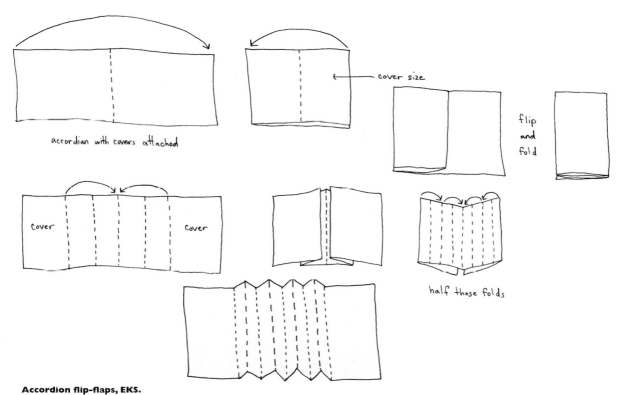

accordian with covers attached

cover size

flip
and
fold

Cover

Cover

half these folds

Accordion flip-flaps, EKS.

Cityscape Instant Accordion

This is one of my silly inventions. As I played with the instant accordion form (which you can see in more detail in How to Make Books*), I realized you could cut some of the lines with designs to make it more interesting. I like to "draw" with my scissors, just cutting whatever shapes occur to me, but you can pencil in your cut lines. (You can erase when the book is finished.) An X-Acto® knife, if you are skillful with it, is another excellent way to do this. You could even cut little windows and architectural details if you get inspired.*

YOU WILL NEED

Foldable, sturdy rectangular paper—use 8½ x 11" (21.5 x 28cm) (or another standard printer/photocopy paper) if you'd like to instant publish via photocopy

Scissors or X-Acto® knife, blades, cutting mat, straightedge, etc.

Bone folder

Pens, pencils, markers, rubber stamps, and collage materials, to embellish as desired

Adhesive

1. Fold the paper in half vertically, and burnish.

2. Fold both edges into the middle fold, then unfold.

3. Fold the paper in half horizontally, then unfold.

4. Very carefully, fold the top to the middle, creasing only the leftmost section (to the first vertical fold on the left)—and crease just a touch on the right edge to indicate the middle. Repeat on the bottom, folding the bottom to the middle and creasing in the same way.

5. On both the top and bottom, cut from the indication mark to the crease made in step 4 in a jagged skyline of rectangles, etc., so that it forms a negative and positive skyline on both the top and bottom quarters. (Alternatively, make this cut curvy for a landscape effect.)

6. Cut the horizontal center fold from the left edge to the last segment—across ¾ of the page.

7. Accordion fold on your pre-folds. When you get to the end of a row, fold down and then continue folding across. A little glue on those fold-downs can help it stand. You should end up with an accordion book that stands on its side with a cityscape or landscape top edge. If you did it wrong, you may have invented something new.

8. Embellish with drawings, rubber stamps, collage, cutouts, and/or pop-ups.

"Downtown," Polly Faust, cityscape instant accordion, collage.

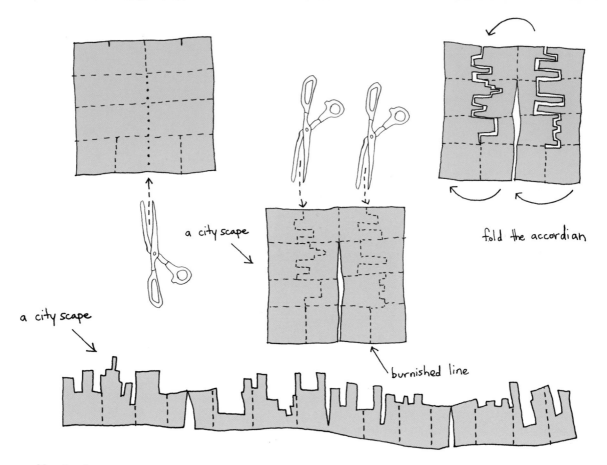

a city scape

a city scape

burnished line

fold the accordian

Variation

For lower pages, just fold and cut in the opposite direction, orienting your paper horizontally.

To publish this via photocopy, make your original on white paper with black lines, collage, stamp ink, etc. Photocopy is not perfect for registration, so don't put anything closer than ½" (1.3cm) to the edge or cuts. Print your copies on any color paper that makes sense with your design. Always test one copy, cutting and folding to see how it looks, before you press the button to print a bunch of them.

Alternatively, with color photocopy or via computer printer, you can scan stuff and use as much color as you like for your original. Check for cracking before you print a bunch on a computer printer—some papers that work for printing just don't fold well. You can try scoring with your bone folder to help prevent cracking.

Resources

Books

Carter, David, and James Diaz. *The Elements of Pop-Up: A Pop-Up Book for Aspiring Paper Engineers.* New York: Little Simon, 1999.
This book shows the hard stuff if you really get into making pop-ups.

Fleischman, Paul. *Copier Creations: Using Copy Machines to Make Decals, Silhouettes, Flip Books, Films, and Much More.* New York: HarperCollins, 1993.
This book has self-publishing techniques and ideas. It's written for kids, but adults can enjoy it, too.

Our Wonder World: A Library of Knowledge (Amateur Handicraft Vol. 7.) Chicago: Geo. L. Shuman & Co, 1926.
My delightful father-in-law, Paul Faust, kept this for 81 years and gave it to me when I was writing this book. Page 86 has a photo of "A Book for Esther to Read"—look for it online or wherever antiques are sold!

Smith, Esther K. *How to Make Books: Fold, Cut & Stitch Your Way to a One-of-a-Kind Book.* New York: Potter Craft, 2007.
My first book, which will walk you through all the basics of bookmaking.

Online

The Movable Books Society
http://movablebooksociety.org/
The Movable Books Society is a group of artists, collectors, and professionals. Their site has links to a myriad of resources.

Robert Sabuda
www.robertsabuda.com
Robert and his staff have been generous about visiting my classes—one of my students became their intern and has now published her own pop-up book. This site has patterns to print out and pop-up.

Canadian Bookbinders and Book Artists Guild
http://www.cbbag.ca/Resource.html
A great resource of resources.

Cooper Union Continuing Education
www.cooperunion.edu
I will be teaching Magic Books and Paper Toys there!

Kate's Paperie
www.katespaperie.com
The boutique of papers. Some of my former students work here, so you know they're well-informed.

School of Visual Arts
www.schoolofvisualarts.edu/ce
Dikko teaches letterpress here, and I'll be teaching Artists' Books classes.

Dikko gave Susan Happersett some strips of brown paper on her way out of Purgatory Pie Press. She started just playing with them on the uptown subway.

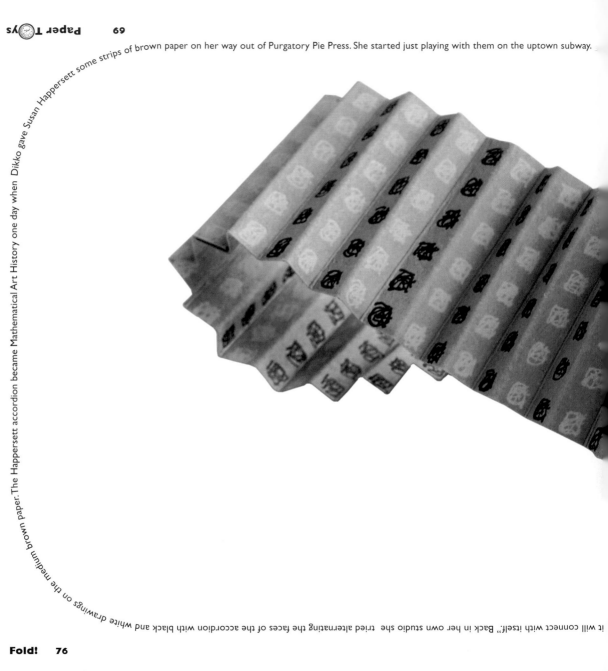

it will connect with itself." Back in her own studio she tried alternating the faces of the accordion with black and white drawings on the medium brown paper. The Happersett accordion became Mathematical Art History one day when

...e pleated one strip into a tiny concertina and twisted it into a moebius. "I thought it was a really great form and the more I looked at it, I realised that if I colored the fo ds in alternating colors, it would look totally different from different angles. Therefore it has two faces, which is kind of special because a moebius, it only has one side—if you take a pencil and draw a line around a moebius

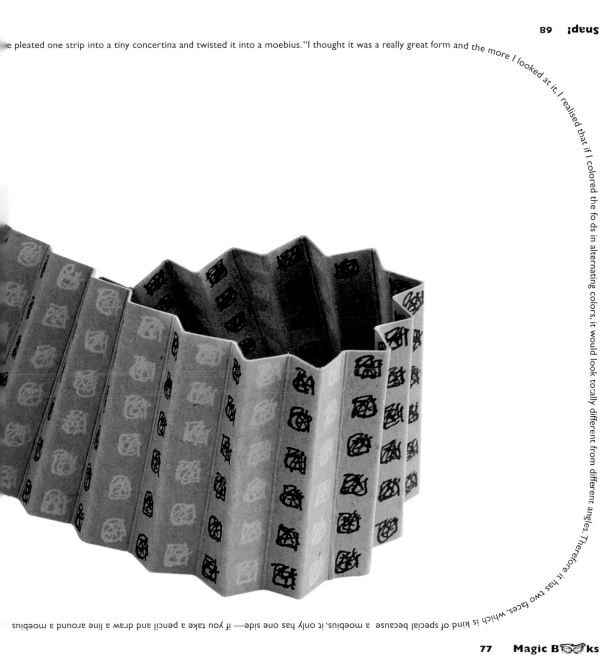

Esther K. Smith

Magic Books &

PAPER

TYS

illos by Liz Zanis

photos by Amy Kalyn Sims

POTTER
CRAFT
New York

Flip Books, E-Z Pop-Ups & Other Paper Playthings to Amaze & Delight

CONTENTS

"Dress Eclectique," Isabelle Deveraux, Purgatory Pie Press. Letter press from linocut and photoengravings, hand set metal type, plastic purse stitched by Liza Jane Norman.

Introduction: Paper Toys

Long before I ever thought of making books, I got a hexaflexagon in the mail from Dikko. Other men send flowers, jewelry, or chocolate, but he wooed me with paper. (It worked—we've been collaborating on art and our family for many years now.)

He had read about them in Martin Gardiner's math column in Scientific American and made one for a grad-school course at the University of Wisconsin. The flexagon was so cool. I made them for a while—sent one to my mathematician cousin (he was not impressed)—and then forgot about them. Years later, teaching a class at Cooper Union called Instant Artist's Books, I found that hexaflexagon again and decided to include flexagons in my class. Then I got a photocopy of a page from a Victorian children's book that showed magic wallet construction. Those two forms were so easy and interesting that I built a curriculum around them. I developed my Magic Books & Paper Toys weekend workshop which started at New York's Center for Book Arts. I've taught it at Long Island University, The San Francisco Center for the Book, and Penland School of Crafts.

When I began teaching design for CUNY, I used flexagons with my CUNY undergrads for design and color-theory problem solving. Since their designs split and reverse, they make an interesting design challenge. They also keep me amused.

I added flip books, strip animations, and spinners with wonderful results. One student rendered a paint can that sprays grafitti, another made a subway car with cut-out windows that show the stations changing.

I've seen flip books of fingernails growing, T-shirts changing designs, and all kinds of winking, blinking spinners. I wish I could see the cool things YOU make!

Left: Purgatory Pie Press Artist Toys series. Right: "The Happersett Accordion," by Susan Happersett, boxed deluxe, letterpress from hand-set type and photoengravings.

4

REVEAL!

F rom sleight of hand to animated pictures—from universal childrens' games to surrealist games—these projects reveal their secrets for hours of amusement.

"Hankerchief," Liz Zanis, Screenprint cootie catcher

Cootie Catcher

You remember cootie catchers, but maybe not how to make them. People always bring them up when I show them flexagons. I didn't take them too seriously—they were so ordinary—but a couple of incidents changed my mind. I met an artist who had made some as part of a performance. I also saw some interesting artists' versions at Printed Matter, the artist book gallery in New York City. And then my children made cootie catchers at a dinner party that included a woman from Italy and one from Japan. Both women were thrilled, remembering the paper toys from their childhoods. At my City University course, someone mentioned cootie catchers, so I went around the room, asking people where they came from—about 16 different countries!—and if they remembered making them. Almost all did (except for the student from Kazakhstan), or remembered their sisters making them. Someone folded one quickly to show people who might not understand what we meant, and two Chinese students got excited. They had made cootie catchers, too, but just didn't know the English word for them. Their version had Chinese characters on the four sides for north, south, east, and west. Inside was a normal fortune teller about love, death, and money. I began to realize that cootie catchers were universal folk form, taught by children to other children.

YOU WILL NEED
One square of writing-weight paper
Bone folder
Pens, markers, etc., to embellish

1. Take a square of paper and fold it in half horizontally. Open. Fold in half vertically. Open.

2. Fold in half diagonally. Open. Fold diagonally the opposite way. Open.

3. Fold all the corners into the center, using your prefolds as guides.

4. Turn the paper over. You will have an unbroken, folded square.

5. Fold all corners into the center again on this side, using your prefolds as guides.

6. Fold in half, making the side you just folded the interior.

7. Pinching the outer triangles on both ends, push together into a 3-D diamond shape.

8. The outside will have open ends. Reverse the folds of the outer layers to open pockets that your fingers will fit in.

9. Place your thumbs and forefingers into those openings, then move them apart and together to manipulate your cootie catcher.

You may wonder why these are called cootie catchers. Warning: This may gross you out (as it did with the person I tried it on). Cooties are lice.

"I Mark This," Polly Faust, fortune teller, rubberstamp on graph paper.

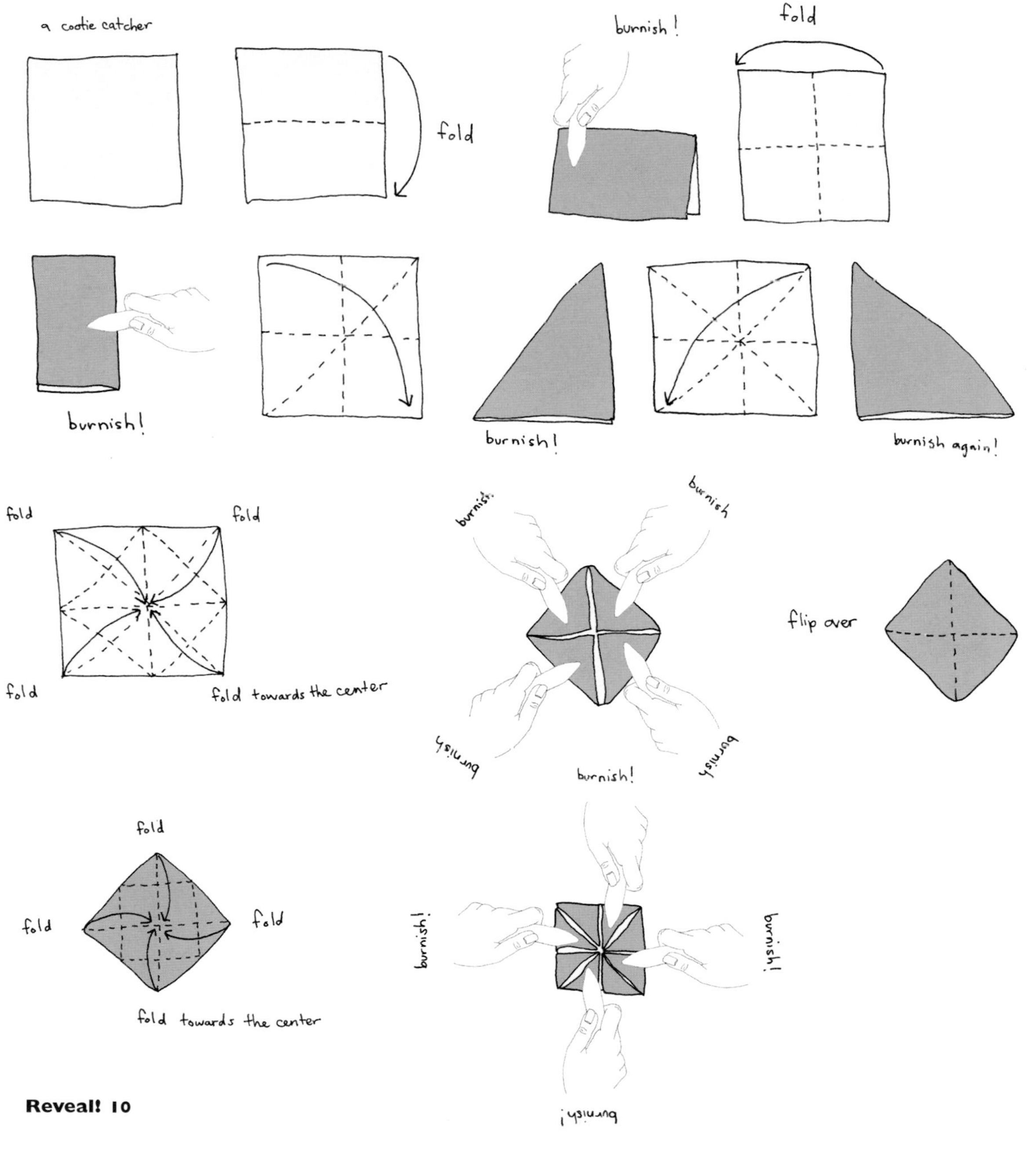

a cootie catcher

fold

burnish!

fold

burnish!

burnish!

burnish again!

fold

fold

fold

fold towards the center

burnish

burnish

burnish

burnish

burnish!

flip over

fold

fold

fold

fold towards the center

burnish!

burnish!

burnish!

burnish!

Reveal! 10

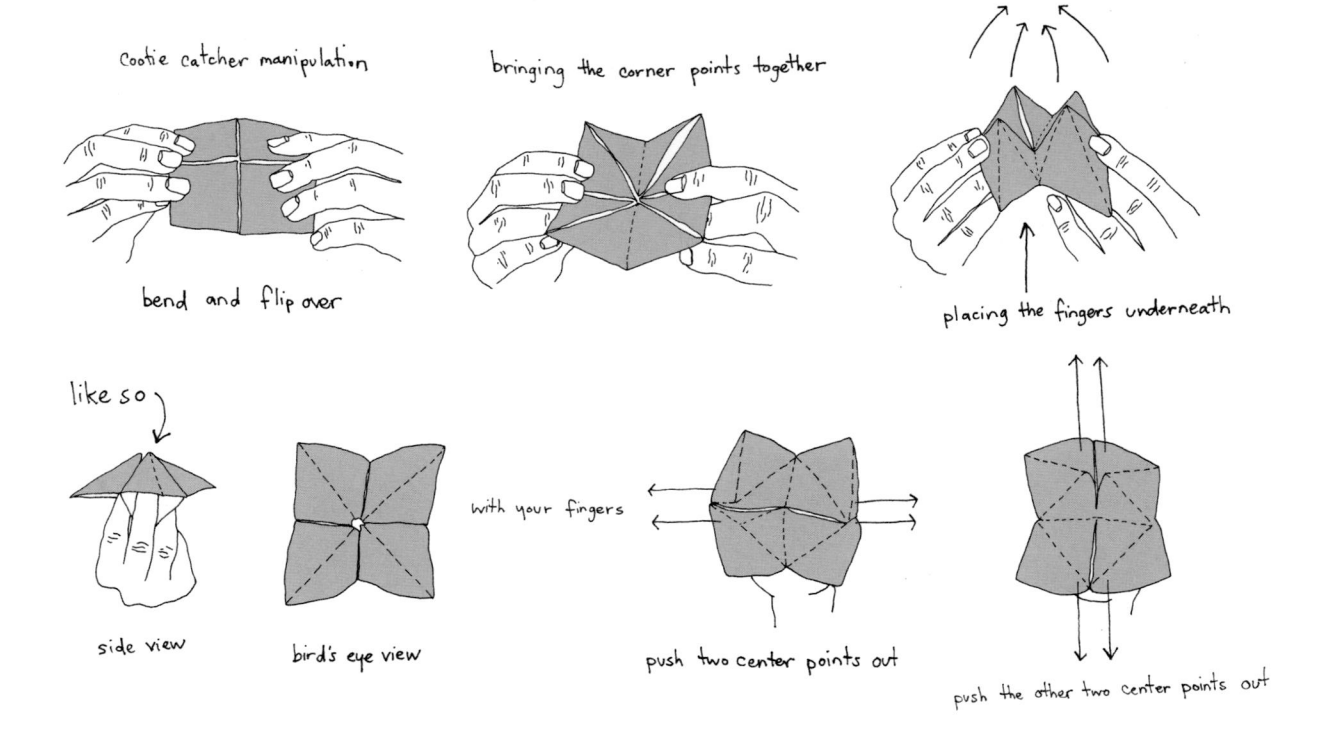

Cootie catcher manipulation

bend and flip over

bringing the corner points together

placing the fingers underneath

like so

side view

bird's eye view

with your fingers

push two center points out

push the other two center points out

10. Take your fingers out and flatten the cootie catcher so that the finger slots are flat on the table, revealing the inside.

11. Observe the four triangles that meet in the center.

12. Opposite triangles are revealed as you manipulate the cootie catcher. Try it and see what I mean.

13. Leave two triangles blank.

14. On the other two, stipple with dots, or draw tiny bugs. I used a pen and quickly scribbled in little legs and small bodies.

Now try it out. Push the triangles together so that the inside is hidden. Open out your finger holes again and place your fingers and thumb inside. It's good to do this one-handed if you can. Then open the catcher in one direction so the plain paper shows. When you open it the other way, the bugs show. Practice so that you can do this smoothly. It's sleight of hand. Approach your friend and show the clean inside. Say, "I'm catching cooties!" Touch his or her hair with the cootie catcher. Then open it the other way so the bugs show. Say, "Ew! Yuck! Look what I got!"

Exquisite Corpse Flap Books

This toy/book/game started as a Victorian children's drawing game that the Surrealists developed. Some are collaborations, others are by a single illustrator. Some include hilarious text, some are just pictures.

YOU WILL NEED
Three pieces of paper
Pencils and other drawing/collage supplies
Three people

1. Have each person draw a head and neck and fold the paper down so only the lines of the neck show.

2. Trade papers, and then have each person draws a torso, indicating where the legs will begin. Then fold the paper so that the torso is hidden.

3. Trade papers again, and have each person finish with the legs. Open the paper up and see the crazy combos.

The Surrealists used this game for both art and poetry. The name *exquisite corpse* comes from a group poem, which was a blind collaboration—one person wrote the subject, the second the verb, and the third the object. Here's that poem:

The exquisite corpse (subject) *Le cadavre exquis*

shall drink (verb) *boira*

the new wine (object) *le vin nouveau*

It's like Mad Libs.

There are several ways to turn this idea into a paper toy. Here is the simplest one.

YOU WILL NEED
Paper
Pencil
Scissors
Bone folder
Straightedge or triangle

Exquisite corpse flap books. Left: "Mr. Harvey's House of Beauty," Harvey Redding and Purgatory Pie Press, letterpress from photoengraving, PurgaColor™, and hand set type. Right: "Kitchen Spirits," Liz Zanis, screenprint.

Paper Tys

1. Fold your paper in thirds, like a letter that you are folding to fit in an envelope. A wasteful, but easy way to do this is to fold the paper in four and cut off one quarter. If your paper isn't long enough to remove a piece of it, you can measure and divide or eyeball it, or roll carefully and then crush your roll for a fold. It doesn't have to be perfect for this try.

2. Now place this vertically on your work table. You need to divide the folded piece into three: the head, the middle, and the tail. These can be even segments or you can make less room for the head, whatever you prefer.

3. Lightly draw two lines using a straightedge or triangle where you want to divide the panel and cut very straight on the lines.

4. Fold the cut flaps over the right panel, lightly trace the flap lines onto that panel as shown, and cut straight on those lines. You should be able to turn the cut pieces and flip-flap them, so that you can mix and match.

5. Now—quick and messy, just to try it out—sketch a head, middle, and tail (or feet) onto the middle, uncut panel. You can also sketch in the lines you will need to follow with the cut flaps.

6. Fold a top flap in, and sketch an alternate head.

7. Fold in the middle flap and add a torso.

8. Fold in the bottom flap and add legs.

9. Repeat 6–8 with the other side panel flaps.

10. Play with your exquisite corpse and see how it functions. Adjust as needed, erasing and redrawing if necessary. When it works, finish your drawings, or make one from nicer paper—90-pound, all-purpose velum will work, as will many other cover-weight or card stock papers. Be sure to fold with the grain. Score if you need to with a straightedge and bone folder.

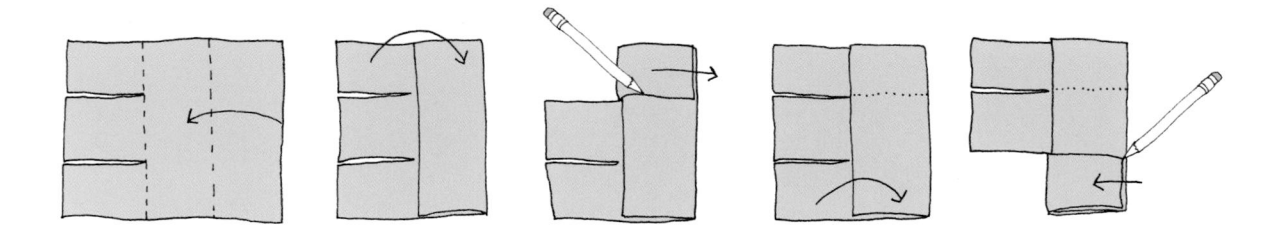

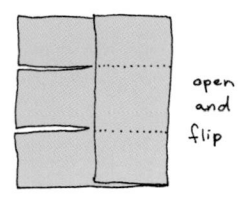
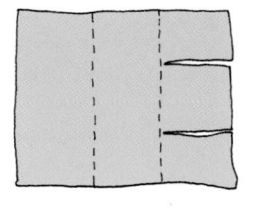 open
and
flip
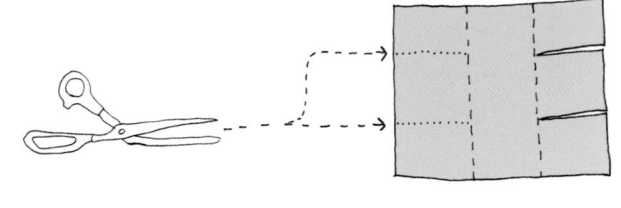

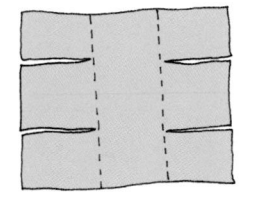

an exquisite corpse

front   back

exquisite corpse variations

Spinners (Thaumatropes)

Thaumatropes are Victorian spinner toys. They work on the concept of afterimage. When viewing alternating images, your brain holds the picture of the first one long enough to combine it with the one on the other side. I have tried light and dark images on these without success. It must be the same on both sides, either both dark on a light background or both white on a dark background for the eye/brain illusion to work. You can see some nice ones on the web when you google Thaumatrope.

YOU WILL NEED

Heavyweight cover paper or board
Cup or compass to trace
X-Acto® knife or sharp scissors
Paper punch
String, or extra-heavy thread
Pencils and other drawing supplies.

1. These do not need to be circles. Squares and rectangles also work, as will any symmetrical shape. If you want a round one, trace a circle from a cup, or use a compass.

2. Cut out your shape with an X-Acto® knife or scissors.

3. Punch two small holes on opposite sides of the circle, each ¼" (0.64cm) or so from the edge. If you need to, trace a circle onto thin paper, cut it out, and fold it in half to use as a guide before you punch.

3. Thread with string, thin ribbon, or extra-heavy thread. Fold the piece in half, insert the loop through the hole, and draw the ends through the loop to secure.

4. Sketch a design lightly on both sides of the circle. The classic thaumatrope is an empty cage on one side and a bird on the other side. The image must be upside down on the back. Both pictures have center lines, and these need to line up with the circle's center.

"EIEIO," Richard McGuire, Purgatory Pie Press, letterpress from photoengraving, linocut, and hand set type.

E·I·E·I·O
1990 RICHARD M. GUIRE
LITHOGRAPHS & PRESS
THE MOTTO 48 N 40 10 1S
EARL GOLD & BANK GOTHIC
TYPES ON MURILLO PAPER
DIKKO, LINOCUT & PRINTER
NO 9 N 1   700# OF 500

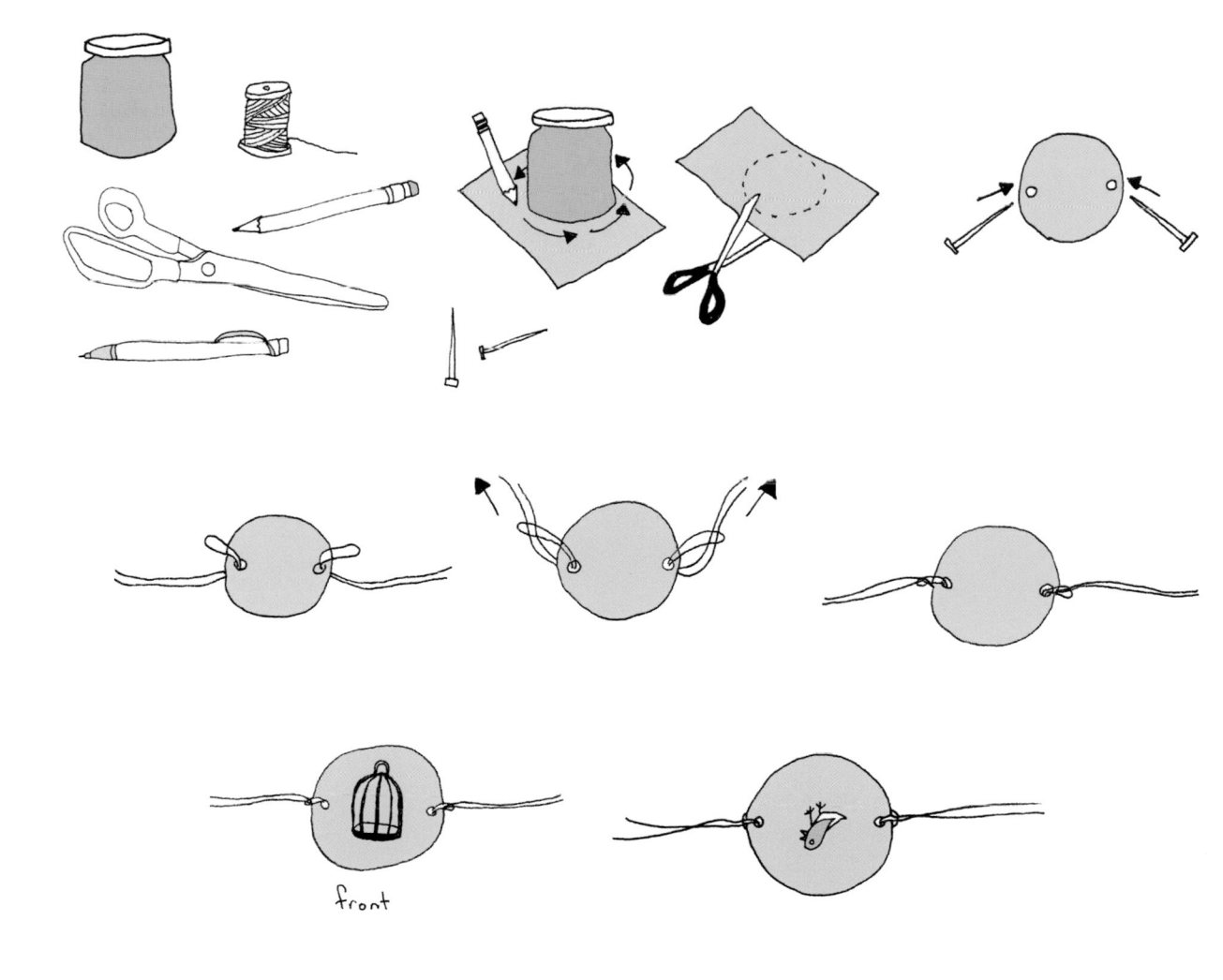

front

5. Spin the disk to see if the animation works.

6. Adjust as necessary.

7. When you've got it, trace over your lines with pen or marker. Make them very high contrast.

8. To operate, twirl the strings between your thumb and fingers. (I figure that is why it's called "thaum," but Greek is not my language.) An alternate way to twirl is to hold both strings and spin the disk so that it winds up, then gently pull back and forth. It will feel stretchy and the disk will twirl one way and then the other for many hours of amusement.

Check out the examples that you find on the web. Old spinners are beautiful, though the riddles aren't as clever as the art!

Once these make sense to you, try some variations: a rubber-stamp critter can go into the cage. And there's no reason not to try some collage! Even an abstract can be nice—play with spinning color mixes, etc. We once made one for a birthday where a starburst appeared over a big number. The corniest ideas can be fun for this toy.

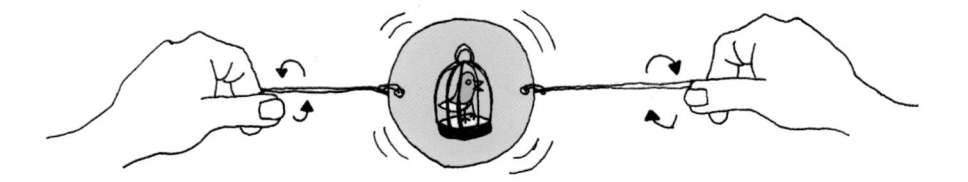

Strip Animations

Moving pictures—now you see them, now you don't.

I saw these in a Popeye comic strip in an old collection—the Sunday funnies included paper toys to keep the kids amused. They are easy and fun to make.

YOU WILL NEED
Paper—cardstock will do nicely
X-Acto® knife
Ruler
Scissors
Pencil and other drawing materials, plus collage materials, rubber stamps, etc.

a dripping faucet

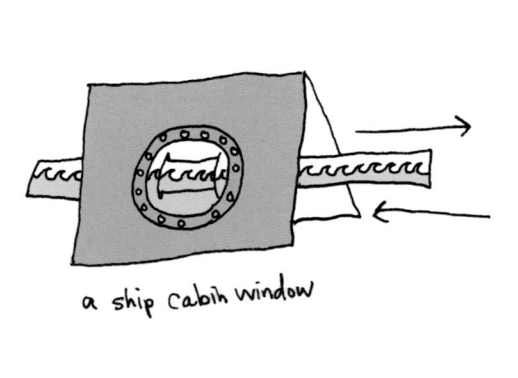

a ship cabin window

an elevator

"Basement Accident," strip animation, Liz Zanis. Background, antique newspaper funnies.

1. Plan a drawing with an element that changes—a TV set, for example.

2. Slit the top and bottom or the sides of the paper, aligned with where the movable element will appear on your paper.

3. Cut a strip of paper to fit through the slits.

4. Include stops so that the strip can't be easily pulled out. To do this, measure a strip of paper slightly smaller than the slits, but at the top and bottom draw a larger shape to keep it from coming out. Weave the strip of paper into the slits.

5. Make sure the strip moves well.

6. Pencil in the "static" image on the card and the moving image on the strip. My favorite one from that Popeye collection was of Wimpy eating a long strand of spaghetti as flies went into his mouth. Running water is also fun. In some, facial expressions or hairstyles change (think Tressy Dolls). In another, Olive Oyl's feet change as she dances the Charleston. See what you invent!

7. When you are happy with your sketch, draw it darker or with pen. You can even add color or collage elements.

you will need :

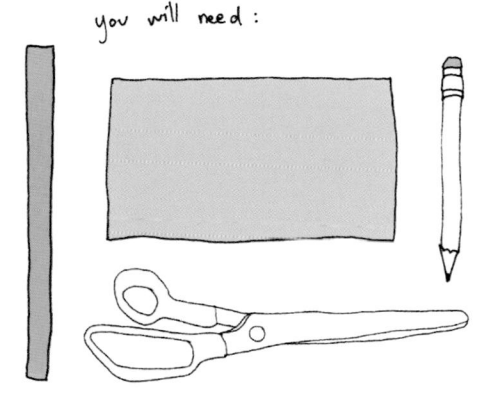

measure the strip width.

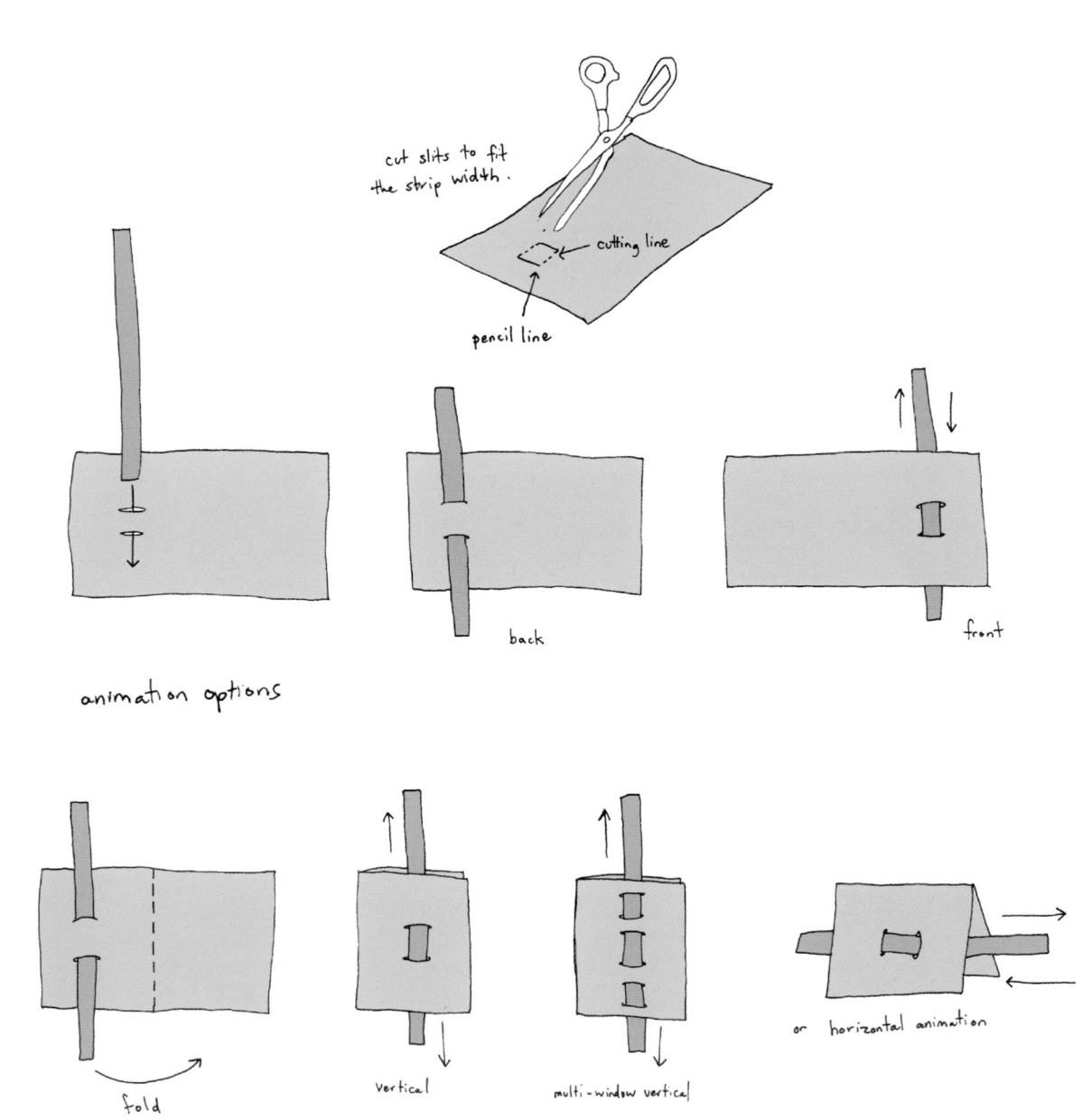

cut slits to fit
the strip width.

cutting line

pencil line

back

front

animation options

fold

vertical

multi-window vertical

or horizontal animation

Rolling Ball

I've seen these made from holiday cards as ornaments, but they are also interesting books. And it's fun to roll them. You could even put a simple pop-up (see page 12 of Magic Books) inside.

YOU WILL NEED
Heavy, foldable paper
Compass or round object (glass, bowl) to trace
Pencil
Scissors
Bone folder
Adhesive
Drawing and collage materials to embellish
Velcro®, magnets (optional)

1. Trace circles onto the paper using a compass, or trace a jar or small bowl. The heavier the paper, the fewer circles.

2. Cut the circles out with scissors or a knife.

3. Fold them in half and burnish.

4. Adhere the folded circles back to back, lining them up with care and burnishing until you have enough to create a full ball shape when you open up the ball.

5. Place Velcro® or magnets on the covers so that the ball can stay open.

6. Roll your book to be sure it works.

7. Embellish with drawing, rubber stamps, or collage.

Rolling Faces

You can put whatever appeals to you on the pages of your rolling book. Faces can be fun. One student thought faces of politicians would be nice rolling away. Cut them from magazines or newspapers and collage.

"The Eye Ball Book," "Just a Kiss," and "About Face," Susan Happersett, rolling ball books, collage.

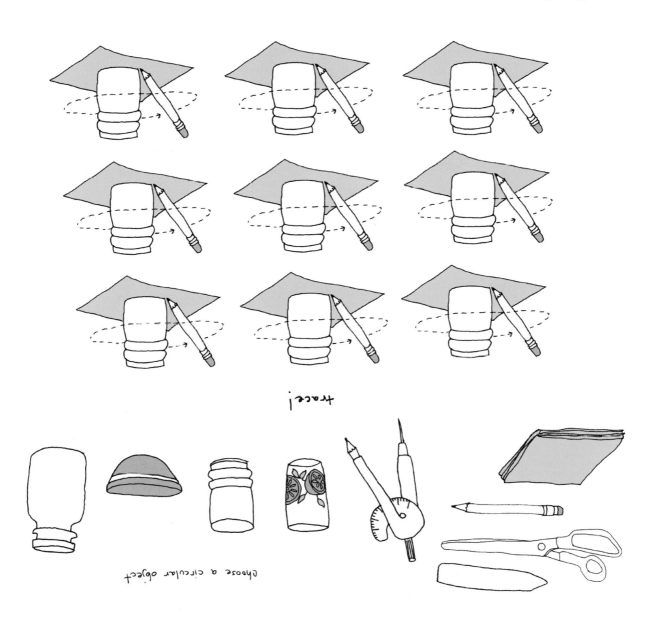

trace!

choose a circular object

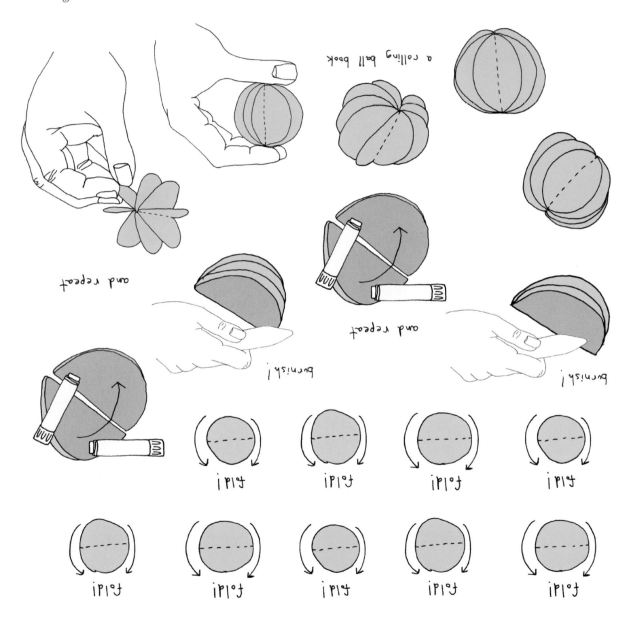

a rolling ball book

and repeat

burnish!

and repeat

burnish!

fold!   fold!   fold!   fold!

fold!   fold!   fold!   fold!   fold!

FLEX!

A Princeton mathematician was doodling with a strip of paper in the 1940s and invented the hexaflexagon. It combined the magic of the number 9, the magic of equilateral triangles, and the magic of Möbius strips. When you turn it inside-out or "flex" it, hidden panels are revealed, and the designs break and reverse. When you get the hang of the precise folding, it becomes pleasantly hypnotic, meditative, and relaxing. When I was first obsessed with making these, a friend came to town, so we showed her how, and all weekend she'd pick up strips of paper and fold them. Our kids were little then, so we'd make them, and the kids would decorate them, and everyone was happy. (Until we had to clear the kitchen table!)

I began to hear about other flexagons. I found some in math books; a student showed me another. I heard that Suellen Glasshausser, an artist who had visited my artist books class at Cooper Union, also loved them. I meant to get together with her sometime and see what she could show me, but I never had the chance. She died suddenly, inexplicably, tragically. I want to dedicate these interactive projects to her memory.

Purgatory Pie Press promo: Square flexagons. Dikko Faust & Esther K. Smith, wood type faces letterpress, assorted paper.

29   **Paper T○ys**

Hexaflexagon

This was my first and is still my favorite. The final folds for these must be precise. A childhood misspent on origami is good preparation for making flexagons. Fold so that only one layer of paper is included in your fold, accordion style (like those Kleenex Flowers for Mother we made in elementary school. If you don't remember those, I'll show them to you in my next book, Central Pennsylvania's Crafts, along with the plastic-bag-on-a–metal-hanger Christmas wreaths we made in Inner City Girl Scouts).

YOU WILL NEED

Paper—something foldable, such as heavyweight cover-weight paper or end strips of printmaking paper, work well
Adhesive
Bone folder
Scissors
30°/60°/90° triangle or protractor (I eyeball it, but that takes nerve)
Pens, pencils, collage materials, gouache, and rubber stamps for embellishing.

1. Cut a long strip of paper using a 1:7 ratio. You will eventually get the hang of this proportion, but to start with, measure a piece 2 × 14" (5 × 35.6cm) or 3 × 21" (7.6 × 53cm). Or get out your calculator (unless you can remember long division—remind me to show you the Dutch version of long division) and divide the length of a piece of paper by 7 to find your width. Round this off to something that works on your ruler. An approximate proportion is fine.

2. The next and trickiest thing you need to do is to make your 90-degree corner into a 60-degree angle. You need to remove 30 degrees. You can do this several ways. Use a protractor or a triangle (it is NOT exactly symmetrical; don't let the 45 degrees fool you!). Or you can eyeball it. That's what I always do. You'll get the hang of it with some practice if you are comfortable messing up a few times while you learn how. Always use cheap paper when you learn a new form!

3. Fold that angled edge diagonally up to the top.

4. Turn over your paper and fold the new edge to the bottom.

5. Keep this up until you have ten equilateral triangles.

6. Count them and fold back the remaining bits—you should have a long, skinny parallelogram. If it is a trapezoid, you have too many or too few triangles.

7. When you are sure you have ten, cut off your extra pieces.

8. Accordion-fold the entire strip again.

9. Adhere the front triangle to the back triangle. This should be a little awkward. If it's really easy to glue, you may have an extra triangle.

"Bureau Doilies," Liz Zanis, hexaflexagon, screenprint.

10. It will become a hexagon with folds and cuts. Burnish well with your bone folder.

11. Manipulate the hexaflexagon so that the cuts are mountain folds and the folds are valley folds. You will need to use both hands.

12. Make the points meet at the bottom, and the top will pop open!

13. Flatten this hexagon and burnish well with your bone folder.

14. Repeat. Take those top points, open them, and bring them around to the bottom. The new top will pop open. Flatten and burnish. You now have three hexagons.

15. Number them lightly and fold again.

One of the most interesting things about these flexagons is that if you flex one and flip the piece over, it has reversed. This is hard to understand on paper, so do this simple trick: Draw a quick circle around the middle—flex it, flip it, and see how the circle has broken. Try adding some distinctive little dots in the center, flex it, flip it, and see where your dots end up.

Some designs are known to work well with these flexagons—but you can make up your own. Basically anything that breaks into threes and sixes works great. Baby blocks are wonderful; designs like flat squares break weirdly. As I always recommend, sketch on a practice piece. Experiment, try things—and when you like something, make a finished piece.

These can be great with rubber stamps or collage. Glue with care—you can't go over those cuts, only the folds—and it's tough to glue over folds. Better to glue things to flat surfaces—let the glue dry before you try to flex.

Try to make the different faces relate to each other. Something can grow or change or mutate for a sort of animated effect. In one of my workshops a student tricked me. She used rubber stamps and scrap paper and stamped fish across the cuts: first the whole fish, then the head on both sides of the cut, and finally the tail on both sides of the cut. She did this by stamping precisely with waste paper under the fold so that it wouldn't print the whole fish. The effect was true magic. I couldn't understand how she made half the fish disappear.

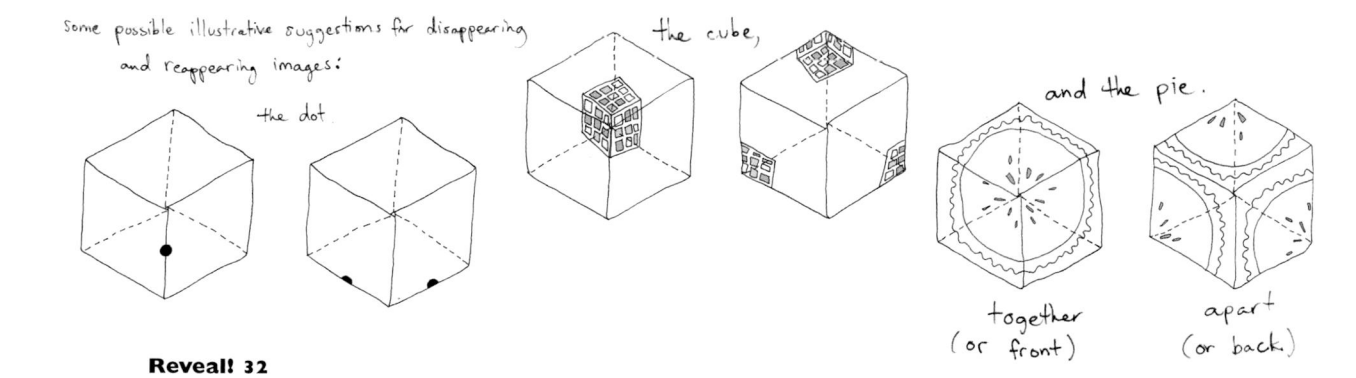

Some possible illustrative suggestions for disappearing and reappearing images:

the dot

the cube,

and the pie.

together (or front)

apart (or back.)

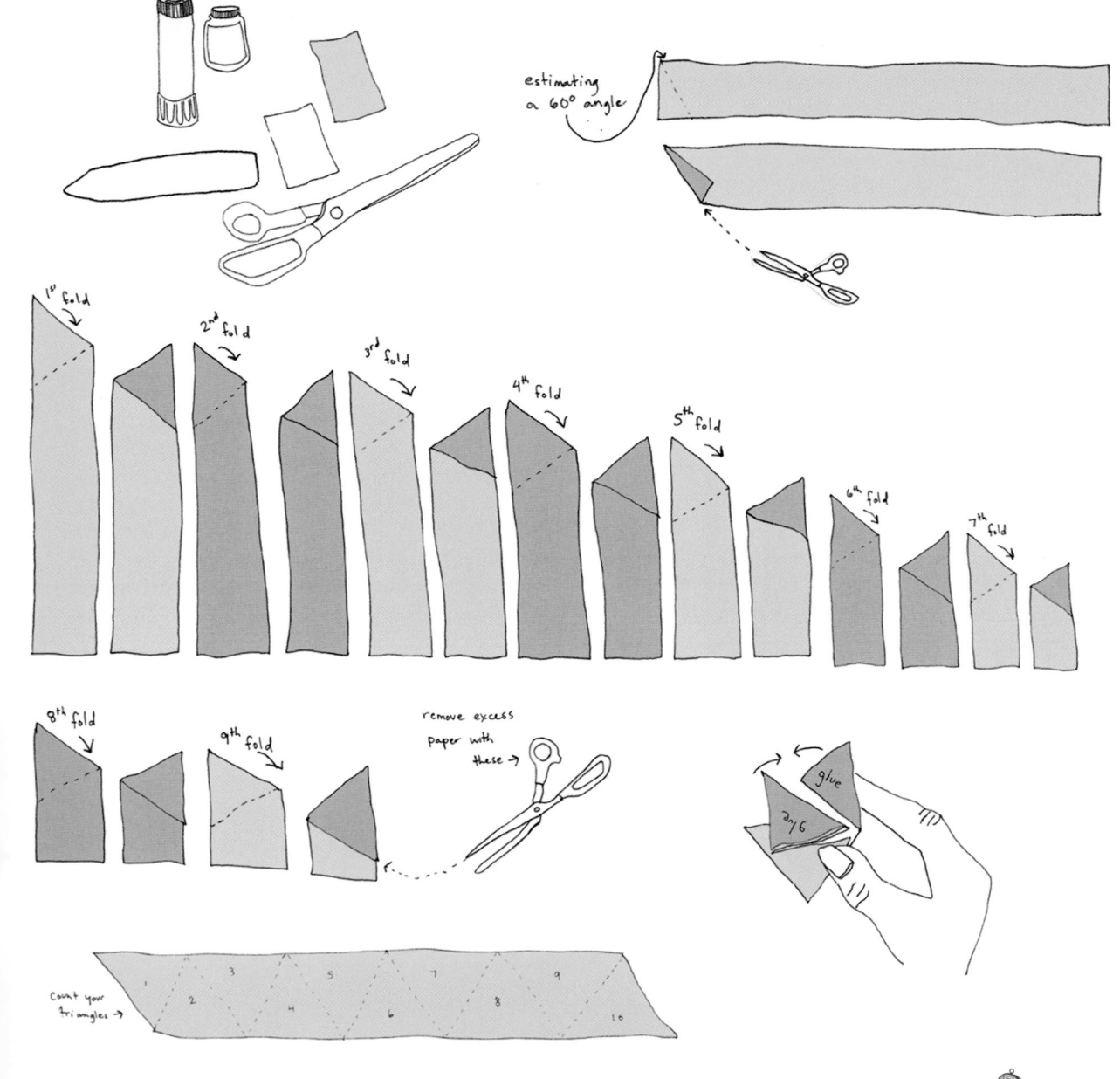

estimating a 60° angle

1ᵘ fold

2ⁿᵈ fold

3ʳᵈ fold

4ᵗʰ fold

5ᵗʰ fold

6ᵗʰ fold

7ᵗʰ fold

8ᵗʰ fold

9ᵗʰ fold

remove excess paper with these →

glue

any 6

Count your triangles →

1 2 3 4 5 6 7 8 9 10

Square Flexagon

This one is easier in some ways than the hexaflexagon—and you can use the square you cut out of the middle to make another flexagon, and a mini flexagon from the inside of that square. Warning: It goes on forever and ever—infinity in motion!

YOU WILL NEED

A square of heavy-weight, foldable cover paper—90 pound works
X-Acto® knife, straightedge, or scissors
Bone folder
Adhesive
Markers, rubber stamps, and other materials to embellish

1. Fold the square in half.

2. Fold both ends to the middle—one to the front and the other to the back as shown.

3. Open and repeat these folds in the other direction. Flatten the paper and you will have sixteen squares marked by the fold lines.

4. Cut out the four middle squares. You can use an X-Acto® knife and straightedge. Or fold in half, cut into the center with scissors, open, and carefully cut out the center with your scissors. If you cut perfectly, you can make a smaller flexagon from this square later.

5. Now you will glue some of the squares together. The gluing is a little tricky. It's best to mark it first as shown.

6. Glue square A to square A, folding the side into the center. Glue square B to square B in the same way.

7. Now, glue square C to square C, folding the side into the center. Glue square D to square D in the same way.

8. This flexagon flexes by folding and unfolding. Fold it in half, open it in the direction it lets you, and keep going. Number the sides lightly so you can tell them apart.

9. Try some designs on a trial version and see how you like them. This symmetry is different from the hexaflexagon—it's simpler. Some sides are vertical, others horizontal. It's fun for faces that become vases. Play with the positive and negative space.

10. When you are satisfied with a design, make a fresh one on nicer paper and paint or collage or draw it with ink. Acrylic and crayons do not work well, since they can mark the other sides of the paper or stick together when you fold and flex. But a little acrylic mixed into your gouache or tempera can give you the best of both worlds—a little smoother and more elastic without the shine and acrylic adhesion. Ink, dry-brush watercolor, markers, and rubber stamps are all excellent for making flexagon designs.

How to Cut a Square from a Rectangle

Most people make squares by folding diagonally, but if you don't want that fold, here is my alternate method.

1. Fold and cut a thin strip of paper across the short side of your rectangle.

2. Use this strip as a ruler. Measure along the long side, and mark the end.

3. Fold at your mark, lining up the top and bottom edges of the paper to keep your fold straight.

4. Cut away the excess strip and voilà! A square.

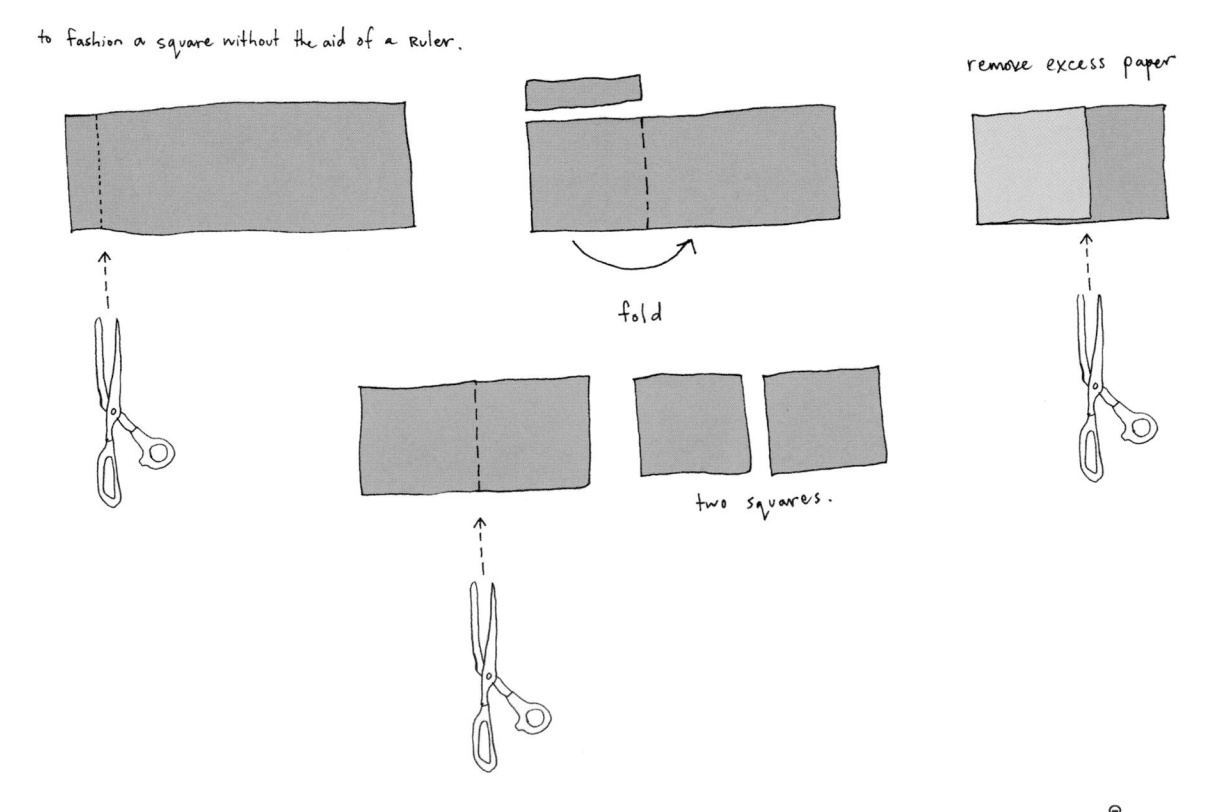

to fashion a square without the aid of a Ruler.

remove excess paper

fold

two squares.

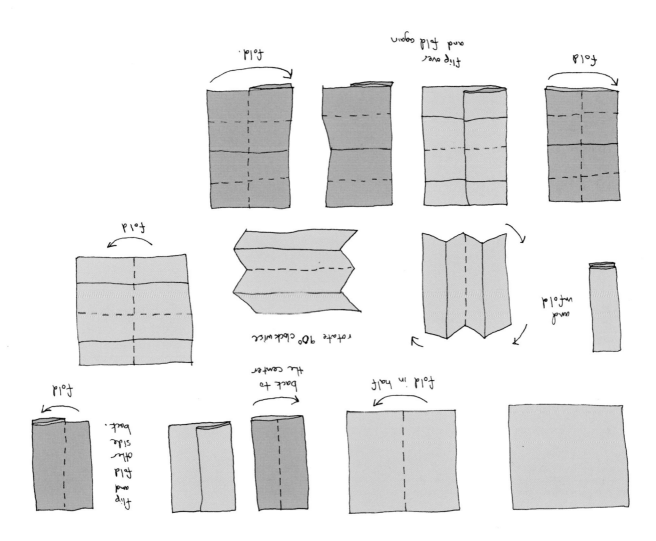

fold.

flip over,
and fold again.

fold

fold

rotate 90° clockwise

and unfold
again.

fold

back to
the center

fold in half

flip and
fold the
other side
back.

fold

glue square "a" to square "a"
and square "b" to square "b"

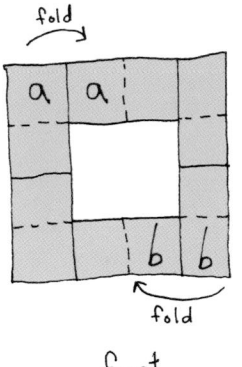

fold

front

fold

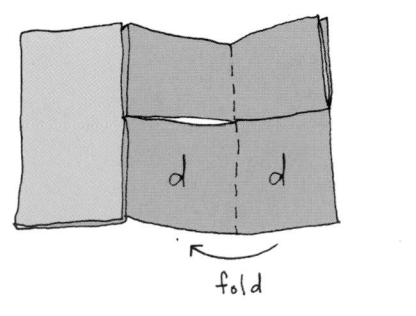

fold

and then flip it over to
glue square "c" to square "c"
and square "d" to square "d"

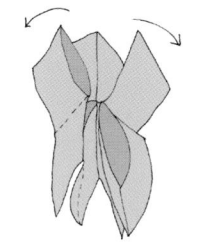

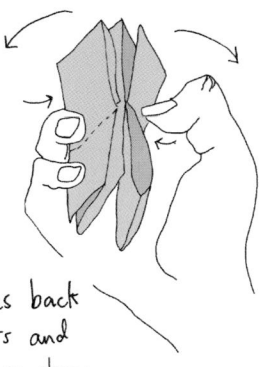

bend the sides back
keeping the cuts and
mountain folds on top.

push in from the bottom
and then the cuts and the
mountain folds at the
top will drop down
and out.

fold

the square flexagon.

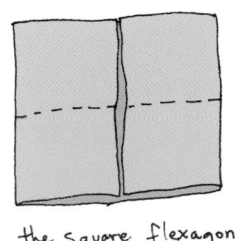

Swiss Cross Flexagon

This is the second flexagon that I fell for—there were others in between, but they just didn't move me. It's the one Suellen Glashauser showed to a friend of mine. I think she called it the Coco Puffs Flexagon—maybe she'd found one in a cereal box. Whatever happened to the prize inside? We need to encourage the food industry to bring those back.

YOU WILL NEED
Two squares of heavy, foldable paper
Bone folder
Adhesive
Markers, rubber stamps, collage, and drawing materials to embellish later

1. Fold both squares in half vertically. Burnish your folds with your bone folder as you go.

2. Fold both ends to the middle, then unfold.

3. Turn your squares 90 degrees and mark the centers in the other direction. You can use one square folded in half to mark the other square. Mark it lightly with a pencil, or bruise with your bone folder—just a little mark on the edge, so you can find the middle.

4. Then fold the other sides into the middle (where there's no middle fold). Make all these folds with both squares.

5. Place the two squares so that their middle folds run opposite each other—one vertical, one horizontal.

6. Glue or tape all four corners together as shown. Burnish well and let dry.

7. Finally, cut. This is the tricky part. Cut one side's middle fold all the way across, being careful not to cut into the other side.

8. When you have finished, turn over and cut the other middle fold. It's almost impossible to do this with without cutting through your first side. To prevent this, cut half way, turn, and cut the other half from the other edge.

9. Now, very gently fold and open to see the sides change. They will form a Swiss cross shape as one of the sides. As always I recommend you number the sides lightly with a pencil so that you understand where everything is.

10. Decorate with symmetrical designs that look interesting from both directions. When you turn the flexagon over and flex from the other side, it all changes—sketch lightly and test your design before you finish.

"Talking with My Closet," Liz Zanis, swiss cross flexagon, screenprint.

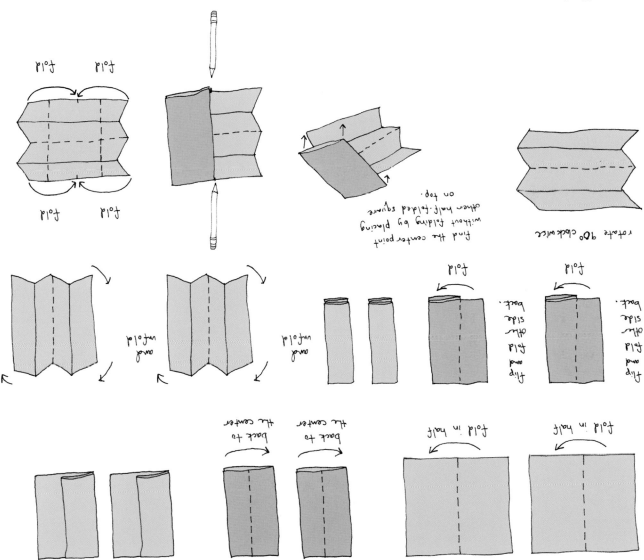

fold   fold

fold   fold

find the center point
without folding by placing
other half-folded square
on top.

rotate 90° clockwise

fold unfold

fold unfold

fold

fold

flip
and
fold
the
other
side
back.

flip
and
fold
the
other
side
back.

back to
the center

back to
the center

fold in half

fold in half

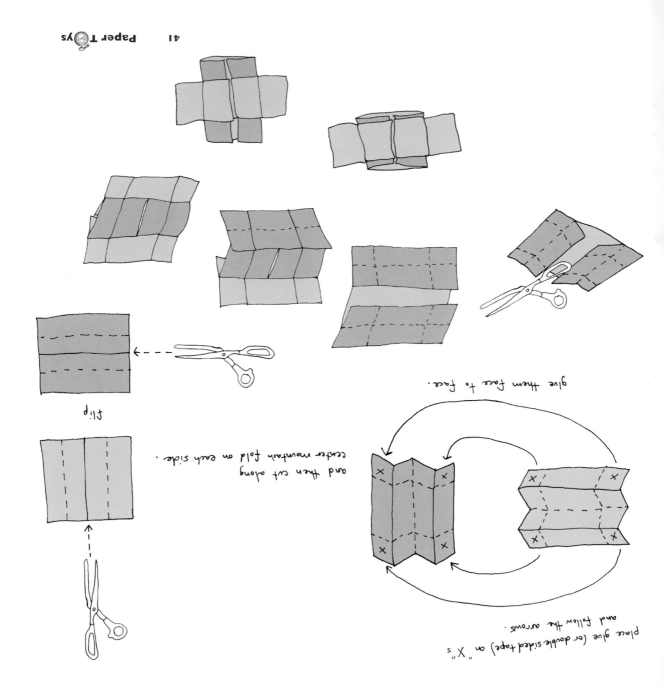

flip

and then cut along center mountain fold on each side.

glue them face to face.

place glue (or double-sided tape) on "X"s and follow the arrows.

PROJECT

NO

TIME

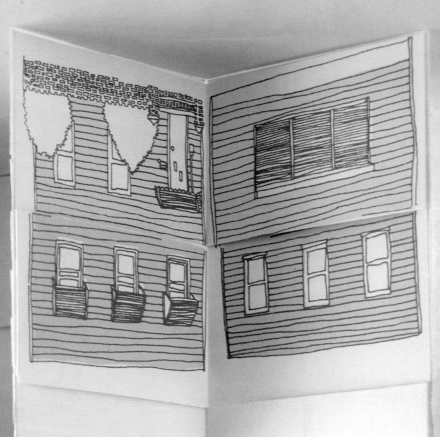

Magic Wallet Flexagon

As I played with magic wallets and flexagons, I began to understand what they had in common conceptually. Both are related to Möbius strips. That is the secret of their magic: the twisted loop where one side is made from two. I don't like glue when it isn't absolutely necessary. I began to think: "What if the strips were the same piece of paper as the covers, with cut-away sections?" And I invented something. It may also have been invented by other people, but it was one of those times when a spark went off. It wasn't quite like that light bulb in the cartoons (more a flash of brain electricity) but it was very cool.

As usual—I want you to try this in some simple, messy way to get the hang of it, and then see what you come up with.

YOU WILL NEED
Paper—8½ x 11" (21.5 x 28cm) is fine to start
Bone folder
Adhesive
Scissors or utility knife and straightedge
Markers, rubber stamps, collage, and drawing materials to embellish later

1. Lay your paper on your work table. Office paper is fine for a quick model. (I quickly pushed some things off my kitchen table and spot sponged it to clear a work space so I could make one to help me explain this to you.)

2. Fold a ½" (1.3cm) tab in, as shown.

3. Fold the bottom up to that tab fold line. Crease and burnish.

4. Then fold that fold to the fold line, as shown. Crease and burnish.

5. Open it up.

6. You need to scribble on this model to indicate which panels will become your covers. Turn the pages so your tab is on the right. Mark the first (left) panel "cover," skip the next panel, and mark the third panel "cover"—you will not cut these.

7. The second panel will be your center strip. Draw the strip in as shown and indicate that you will cut away the top and bottom—the yellow area.

8. Your fourth panel and tab will become your top and bottom strips. Sketch them in and indicate what you will cut away.

9. Now take your scissors and cut away the top and bottom of your second panel and the middle of your last panel/tab.

10. Now for the trickiest part: folding. Fold the first panel/cover under that middle ribbon.

Magic wallet flexagons: Left: "Neighbors," Liz Zanis, screenprint. Right: "Time Is NO Object," Purgatory Pie Press promo, letterpress from handset type and found engravings.

Paper T⊙ys

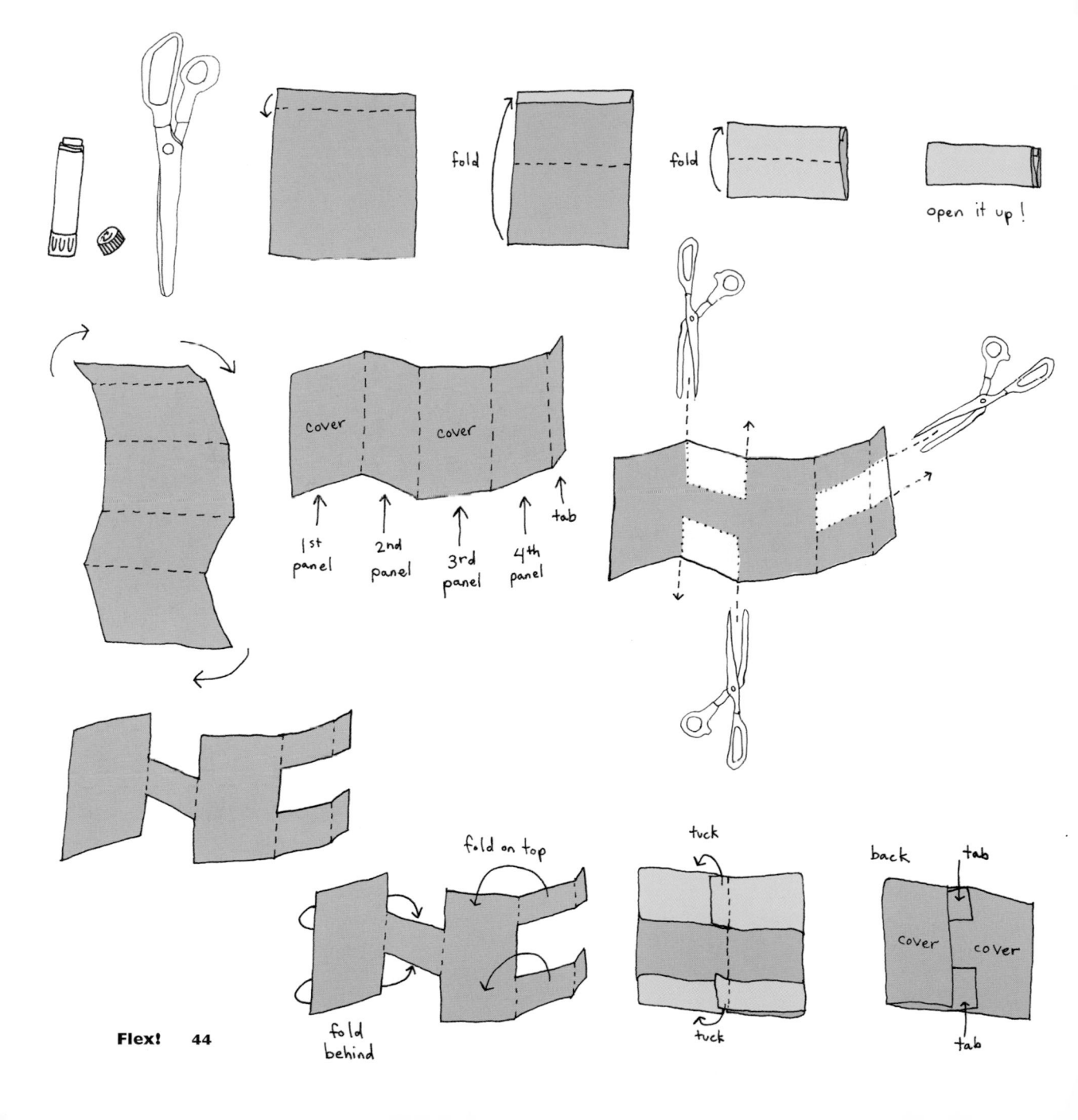

fold

fold

open it up!

cover

cover

1st panel

2nd panel

3rd panel

4th panel

tab

fold on top

fold behind

tuck

tuck

back

tab

cover

cover

tab

Flex! 44

11. Fold the last panel/tab strips over the third cover/panel.

12. Tuck the tabs behind the first panel/cover.

13. Fold the first panel/cover down over the other cover. (You are closing your magic wallet.)

14. Fold those tabs over the outer cover. Affix the tabs to the cover with a spot of glue. For this quick one, a glue stick is fine. Burnish and play with it. Open left and open right. See what you can do with it.

15. Now make one from nicer paper—a foldable, cover-weight paper (approximately 90-pound) is good for this. The proportion of the paper can vary—anything that is pleasing folded into quarters will work.

This toy can be a nice greeting card. Or make covers the size of a check or dollar bill for a version of the magic wallet gift holder (page 64).

Once you've got the hang of it, you can make the ribbons all kinds of funny shapes. Just be sure that the middle ribbon doesn't overlap the top and bottom ribbons or it will "bind" and tear instead of opening and changing smoothly.

See what you can come up with for content. One person used this form to write her friend's favorite Robert Louis Stevenson poem—the first verse appeared if you opened it one way, the second verse when you opened it the other way.

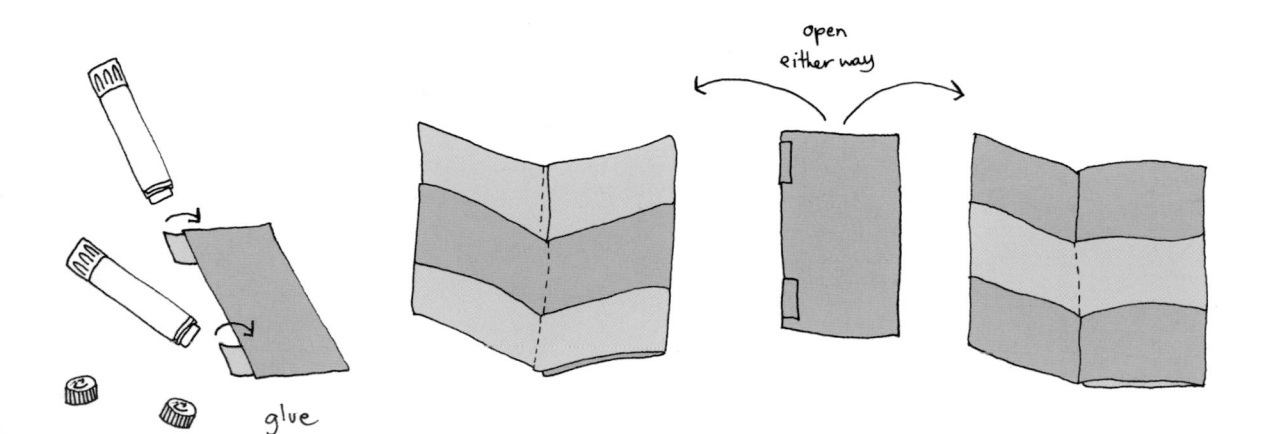

open
either way

glue

Jacob's ladder Accordion Flexagon

This is an odd one! When you weave cards into a slit accordion, it magically opens several ways.

YOU WILL NEED

A few postcards, all the same size
One long strip of short-grain paper the same height as the postcards and slightly more than four times as wide
Scissors
Bone folder

1. Fold the strip into an accordion so there are at least four panels that are a hair wider than the postcards.

2. Unfold the front and back panels.

3. Cut the middle sections horizontally with three cuts, making four strips. Do not cut the front and back panels.

4. Unfold the accordion. Weave the postcards into this paper "warp" as shown. The cards are the "weft" and should alternate (as any weaving would) on that slit accordion warp.

5. Now for the magic: Fold the book closed, then gently open it. When you separate the cards, a secret section is revealed!

6. You can reverse your folds to have it open from the back.

NOTE: This project works with just two postcards, but you can make a longer accordion using more if you like. If you do make a long one, you can make a variety of shapes as you open and shut this toy—have fun playing with them.

Once you understand this one, create a plan using any size cards you like, cutting them from the paper of your choice. Then see if you can come up with a text for this toy!

"Good Luck Flexagon," Alice Austin, Jacob's Ladder Flexagon, ink jet print.

Variation

The slits do not have to be straight. Try cutting them wavy or zigzag for other versions. Try combining colors in an interesting way. And as for content, this project is a great form for a text with a secret or subtext, or the visual equivalent of a story inside a story. Think mystery!

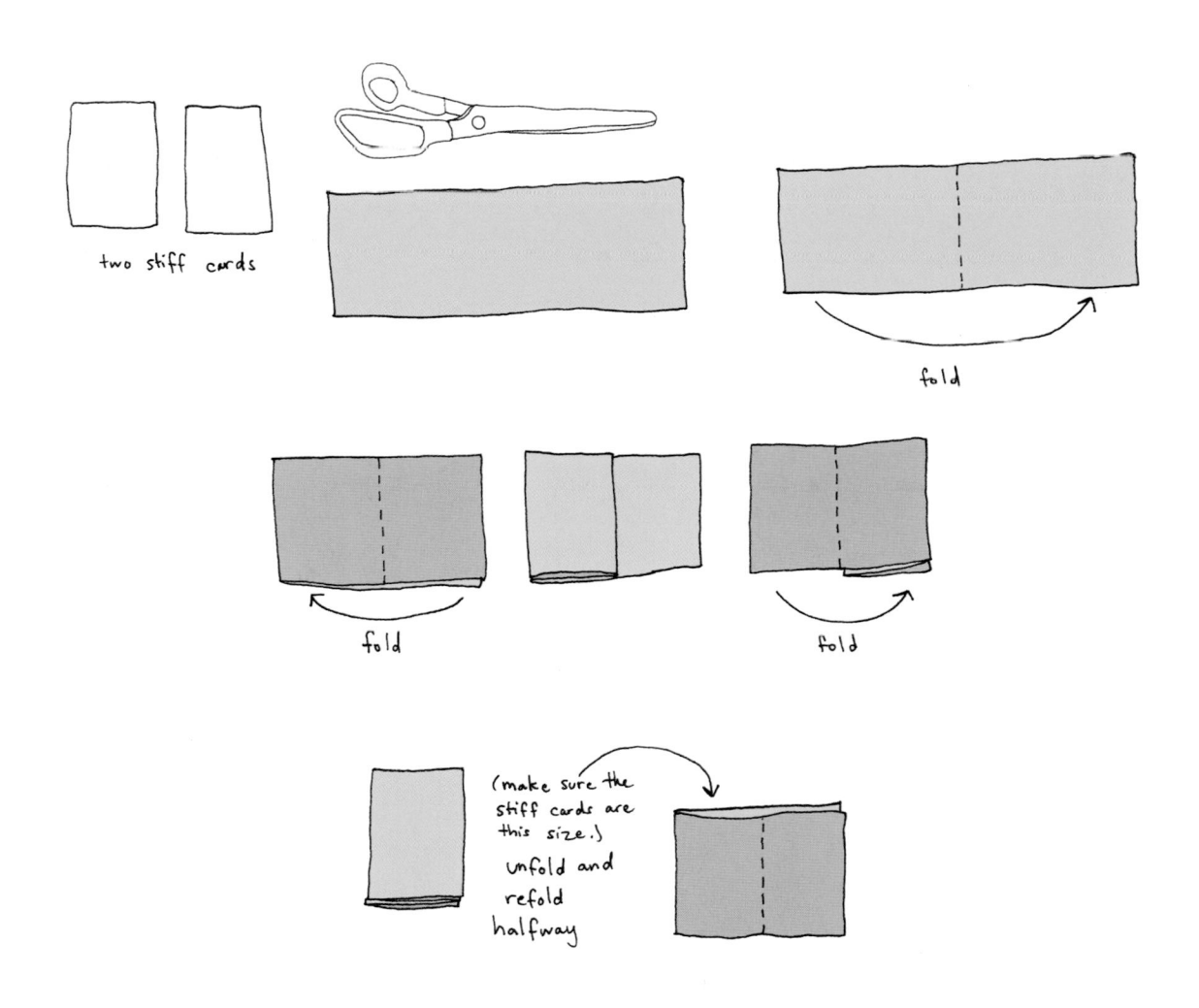

two stiff cards

fold

fold

fold

(make sure the stiff cards are this size.)
unfold and refold halfway

cut along to four dotted line

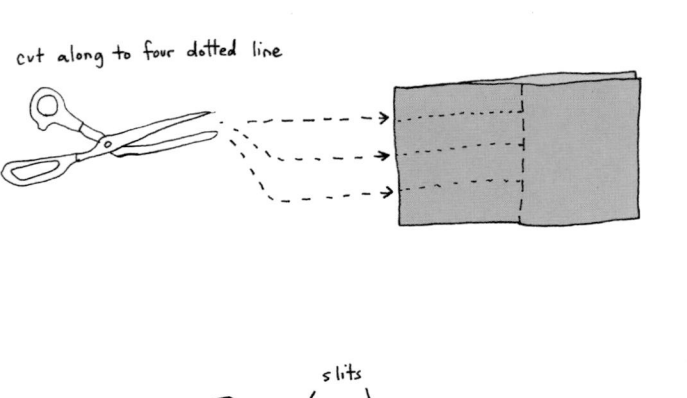

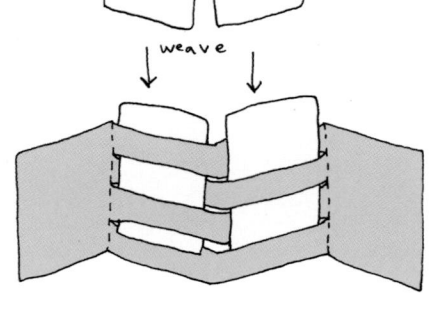
weave

unfold

slits

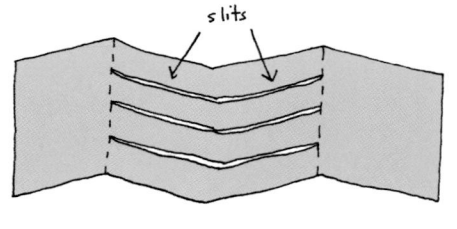

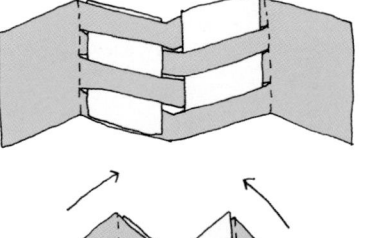

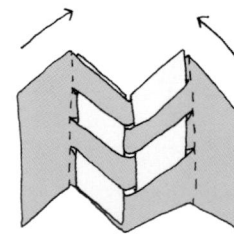
flip to
the other side

to
other side

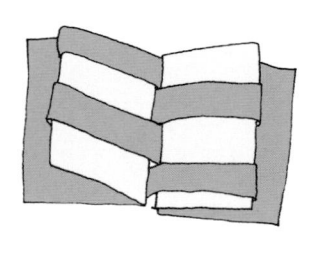

Woven Hearts

These little nonadhesive baskets or pockets fascinate me. You can make the folk-arty ones and even add hangers to use them as candy-filled ornaments, or vary your cuts and end up with something op-arty and interesting.

YOU WILL NEED

Two long strips of strong paper in contrasting colors—3½ x 11" (8.9 x 28cm) is a good basic size, though something else of that proportion will work
Scissors
Bone folder

1. Fold both strips in half horizontally as shown.

2. Round the corners on the top open edges. You can trace around a cup if you need a pattern.

3. Lay the two pieces together in a V shape, so it looks like a heart. Notice that the bottoms overlap in a square.

4. Lightly mark where the bottoms meet. You can use your bone folder for this, or a pencil.

5. Make two cuts into each folded strip from the bottom, a little higher than the square, about 4" (9cm) from the folded edge, creating three loops on each strip.

6. Start weaving the innermost strips. Weave around and through the inside of the loops of the contrasting strips as shown.

7. Repeat step 7, so a checkerboard pattern emerges.

8. When you finish, adjust your strips, finagling them so that they fit together nicely. Squeeze them together from the sides and see how this piece opens into a little pocket basket

9. If you like, glue on another folded strip into the top V of the heart for a hanger.

10. Fill with secret notes or small treats.

"Schmittens," Liz Zanis, woven screenprint. Woven hearts, EKS.

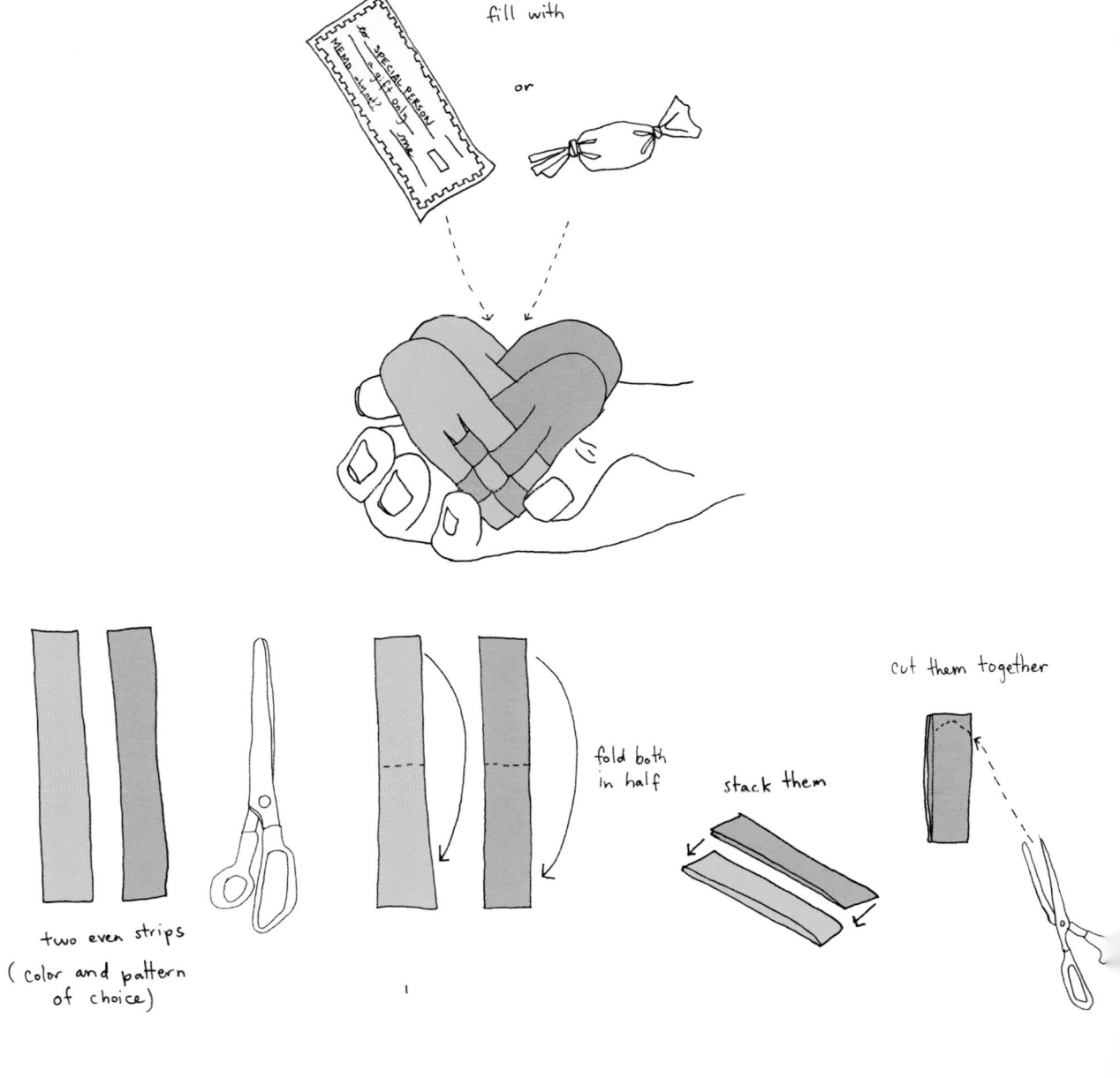

fill with

or

fold both
in half

stack them

cut them together

two even strips
(color and pattern
of choice)

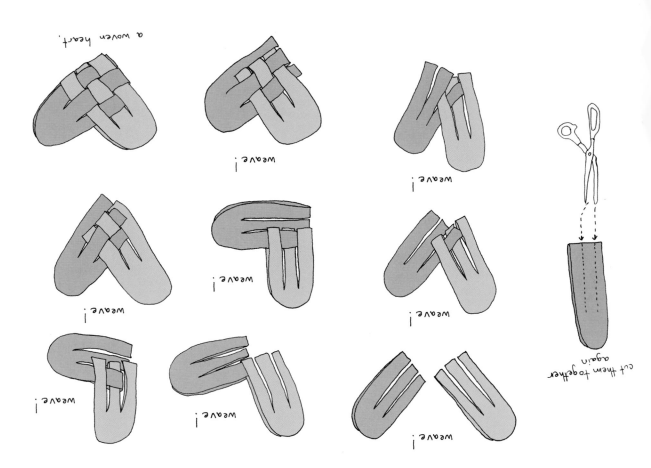

weave!

weave!

weave!

weave!

weave!

weave!

weave!

weave!

a woven heart.

cut them together
again

Op-Art Variations

Once you know how to make the classic woven heart, try some variations. You can cut as many slits as you like (within reason; paper will be weak if you cut it very thin).

You can also cut the slits unevenly, or in curves or zigzags for a different effect. And of course the tops do not need to be curved in the traditional heart shape. They can go straight across or be pointy or be cut in a concave curve for a more modern look.

Black and white strips woven together work very nicely for an op-art woven pocket.

For these and for the traditional woven hearts, you can adhere a folded strip of paper to the top if you'd like a hanger. If you want to hang hearts on a Christmas tree, Swedish-style, this is the way to do it.

Op art woven pocket, EKS.

SNAP!

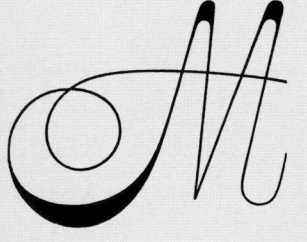

agic wallets are one of the forms that started me down the road that led to this book. I love them. I've been making these for years now, but they are still mysterious. Their secret is that, like flexagons, they are based on Möbius strips. If you use ribbon or paper strips that have two different sides, you will see this.

Magic wallets, EKS, multi-recycled PurgaPaper.

Classic CrissCross Magic Wallet

Start with this traditional version of the Magic Wallet.

YOU WILL NEED

Two identical pieces of binder's board or cardboard—to get started, shirt board, cereal boxes, or anything you have handy is fine

Grosgrain ribbon or twill tape or strips of paper

Glue stick, glue, or double-stick tape—never use rubber cement or masking tape

1. Lay your board pieces side by side, long sides together with a little space in between.

2. Lay four ribbons over them so that the ribbons run straight across the top and bottom of one board and crisscross at the middle of the other board as shown.

3. Adhere the ends of the ribbons to the backs of the boards, wrapping the ends that overlap onto the adjacent boards around the backs, as shown on the following page.

4. Now, test your magic wallet. It should open on both the left and right sides (though it won't turn inside out).

5. Put a piece of thin paper on the ribbon side and close the magic wallet.

6. Open it from the other side. Magic! The paper is now under the ribbon.

7. Close and open from the opposite side. More magic—the paper has moved from one side to the other.

8. If you like your basic magic wallet, you can finish it by adhering some paper on the back to hide the ribbon ends—or make another one or two for practice really quick. Or (if you are really sure you understand it) go on to one of the following projects or variations.

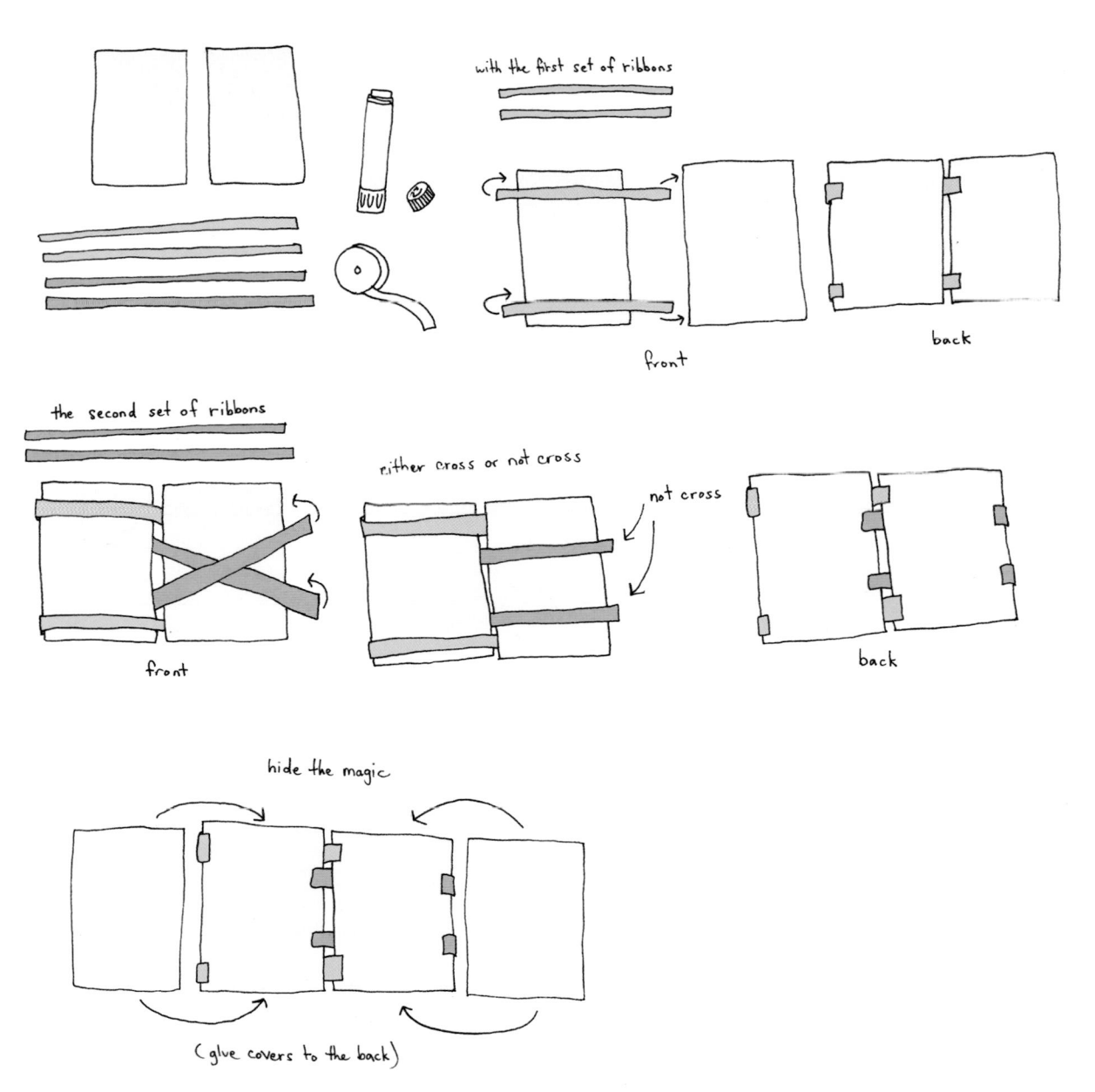

with the first set of ribbons

front

back

the second set of ribbons

either cross or not cross

not cross

front

back

hide the magic

(glue covers to the back)

Snap! 60

Balsa Wood Cover Variation

You can substitute balsa wood for boards for the cover (as seen in the photo on page 59). It cuts with a straightedge and utility knife in the same way. Four thin pieces would work—use two for the insides, attaching the ribbons to them, and then adhere the other two to the outsides to hide the works. You can decorate the balsa wood with photocopy transfer.

YOU WILL NEED

Fresh photocopies of old engravings, or whatever seems nice
Paint brush
Clove oil (available in some health food stores if you can't find it elsewhere)
Balsa wood
Bone folder
X-Acto® knife, straightedge, and cutting mat

1. Paint the clove oil onto the backs of the photocopied images.

2. Place the images front down on your balsa wood.

3. Burnish with a bone folder.

4. Let dry and air out until the smell isn't so strong.

5. Trim the balsa wood to the desired size with an X-Acto® knife and straightedge.

6. Strips of thin suede could work as ribbons with these balsa wood covers.

photocopy transfer

← balsa wood

← fresh photocopy

← transferred image

Modern Magic Wallet Variations

In modern variation of the magic wallet, the crisscross isn't necessary. You can do other things instead. I've used magazine paper strips (folded around themselves for strength) in various configurations over raw board, and let the backs show the "ribbon ends," which I made interesting-looking (in a sort of punk way). Play with it and have fun. The strips can be very wide as long as they don't bind against each other when the wallet is in motion. If the strips are two-sided, then when you open the wallet the other way, you see the backs. This can spoil the illusion—or make it more interesting.

Paper "money" can be a picture that reveals itself in different ways. A student of mine once used a picture from a dance magazine, a naked male dancer looking over his shoulder (no full frontal nudity—it was only R-rated). When the top and bottom were covered, the strips hid his face. When the middle was covered, you saw his face looking over his shoulder with a "come hither" expression—it was hilarious and wonderful.

Magic Wallet Business Card Holder

For this nifty item, you will learn to cover boards with paper or cloth. You will cover the insides, then attach your ribbons, and finally cover the outsides to hide your ribbon ends.

YOU WILL NEED
Binder's board (see step 1)
X-Acto® knife, straightedge, and cutting mat or board chopper
Cloth to cover boards
Adhesive
Grosgrain ribbon or bookbinder's linen tape or elastic
Decorative paper or cloth for finish

1. Cut two covers from binder's board a little bigger than your business cards. The insides of framing mats work well for this. Your local framer may sell them cheap or even give them to you. Museum board is archival if that is important to you. Make them both the same grain. Bounce the board gently between your hands to feel its grain.

2. Cut book cloth or paper a bit larger than your covers—you need about an extra ¾" (2cm) on every side.

3. Center your board on the covering paper and adhere. You may want to line all this up with a metal edge ruler, but eyeball it if you like.

4. Fold the top and bottom paper edges over your board, burnishing with a bone folder. Protect the cover with waste paper so the bone folder doesn't shine it.

5. Open, and then fold the sides in the same way.

6. Open again and cut away the corners of your cover material. There are many methods for doing this, and eventually you'll find the one that works best for you. Basically, you need to cut away bulk but leave enough to cover the edges of the board. Look at your cover and board closely—see how the thickness of the board shows on those fold creases? Trim at a 45-degree angle, leaving that edge to cover the board thickness.

7. Adhere the top and bottom of the material to the board. Burnish well.

8. Adhere the sides of the material to your board. Burnish well again, and pay attention to covering the corner board edge.

9. Arrange the ribbons. Elastic works well for this card holder because it allows for varying amounts of business cards. Elastic won't last forever. The rubber loses its stretch eventually—but you can make a new one in a few years. You may want a change by then anyway. You could also use grosgrain ribbon. Use linen book-binding "tape" (not the sticky kind!) if you are going super-archival.

The side you covered will be the inside of your magic wallet. Arrange your ribbons as on page TK, adhering the ribbons around the backs (unfinished side) of the covers.

10. Attach end sheets. Cut paper just a little smaller (⅛" [0.32cm] or so) than your covers and adhere it. Even a business card could work for this!

11. If you'd like cloth on the outside, you need to deal with the raw edges, unless you like their look. You can cover a very thin board or heavy paper (like a business card) with cloth as you did for the inside, and glue that onto the cover—use a thinner piece of board for the original board, too so it doesn't get too bulky. Bulkiness is a matter of taste. Play with some options and see what you like best.

hide the magic with more cloth!

For this version, you will use heavy, foldable paper, approximately 90-pound cover. I have my students buy pads of this in an all-purpose Bristol vellum finish.

This gift holder magic wallet needs two identical long strips of short-grain, heavy paper. The gift I'm thinking of is either a check or a $1 or $100 bill. If you use a $100 bill, consider making a hole for Ben Franklin to peek through. Currency from other nations is sized differently, so alter appropriately for your gift.

YOU WILL NEED

Paper
Scissors
Bone folder
Waste sheet
Ribbons (grosgrain) or paper strips
Adhesive
Drawing or collage materials for later embellishing

1. Cut two covers, each a little wider than the bill and twice as long, plus a little extra. How much extra? It's your choice—½" (1.3cm) or so gives you ¼" (0.64cm) on all sides, but it could be more if you like.

2. Fold these in half so that they are just slightly larger than the bill.

3. Unfold your covers and line them up long side to long side. You will make your magic wallets with the bottom halves of the paper and eventually fold the top halves down to cover the ribbon ends.

4. Arrange your ribbons or strips of strong paper in the traditional manner (see page 66), or using your own variation, on the bottom halves of your covers, as shown.

5. Adhere the ribbon ends around the backs of your covers (see page 66).

6. Fold down the top halves of the covers to the backs to cover the ribbon ends.

7. Adhere and voilà—covered!

8. Put a check or bill in the middle and test it to be sure it works (try this before gluing your covers).

9. Decorate or embellish with drawing, painting, a note, collage—whatever appeals to you.

"Original Document," Liz Zanis, magic wallet gift holder, silkscreen.

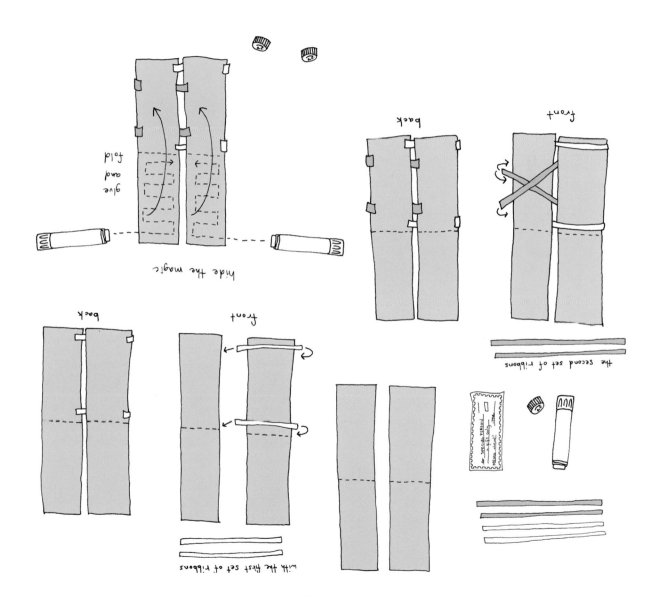

hide the magic

glue
and
fold

back front

the second set of ribbons

back front

with the first set of ribbons

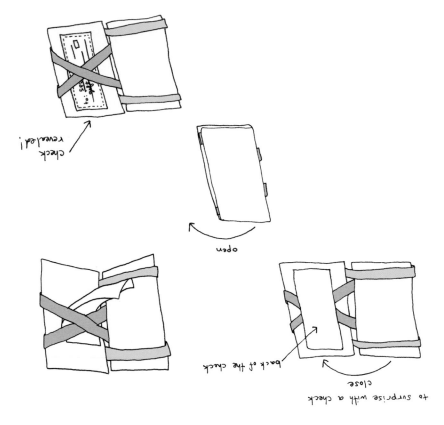

check revealed!

open

back of the check

close

to surprise with a check